About the Authors

Andrew Bondy (@assholevegan) was born in Windsor, Ontario, to a man and woman who prefer to remain nameless. He has never been married but he is really trying. After obtaining an unrelated degree from the University of Windsor, he set off on the highway to learn more about Canada. That search ended in Toronto. Andrew's previous Internet accomplishments are the Babies in Handcuffs Podcast, a mixtape from his hip-hop crew Big Rap, and a video of him playing acoustic guitar on Facebook.

Ren Bostelaar (@renbostelaar) is a writer and photographer who grew up in two Ontario towns that are not Toronto. He's visited every province except New Brunswick, which is technically the same as visiting every province. He received the lowest grade of his university career in statistics. Ren can determine if any television show or movie is Canadian within three seconds.

Julia Davidovich (@juliadavidovich) is a writer/editor who has read maybe three or four books. While native to Toronto, Julia currently resides in Los Angeles—she gravitates to smoggy atmospheres with dense, soupy air. Currently at a length of 175 cm, Julia can be recognized by her red fur and beak-like nose. She typically feeds on insects, crab meat, kale, quail eggs, and occasionally ham. Julia owns zero pairs of snow boots and would like to keep it that way.

Megan Fraser (@meganfraser) is a stand-up comedian/writer originally from Calgary, Alberta. She moved to Toronto in 2004 to follow her dream of becoming an actor, and after failing to book a Tim Hortons commercial, she decided to pursue makeup artistry. When she's not doing any of those things, she's probably procrastinating doing those things. She also failed Canadian history in high school.

Sam Montgomery (@sammontgomery) is the first twentysomething to still be living with her parents. She enjoys collecting books about Princess Diana, smacking herself in the face when the Leafs play, and crying during the Canadian anthem. She disdains long walks on the beach, loves men in denim shirts, and thinks your golden retriever is handsome.

Eric Taylor (@erictaylorswift) currently lives in Toronto, Ontario, with his wife and daughter. Eric is among the tallest Canadians alive, at 196 cm, and one of the only remaining humans with the bloodline of the elusive Sasquatch. During the twelve years he played hockey Eric was awarded a total of twelve participation awards. His ideal Canadian has the raw talent of Wayne Gretzky, the enchanting voice of Shania Twain, the apathetic attitude of Avril Lavigne, and the bushy moustache of Wendel Clark circa 1994.

STATS
Canada
SATIRE ON A NATIONAL SCALE

From the experts behind the Twitter sensation
@stats_canada

PENGUIN
an imprint of Penguin Canada Books Inc.

Published by the Penguin Group
Penguin Canada Books Inc., 90 Eglinton Avenue East, Suite 700, Toronto, Ontario, Canada M4P 2Y3

Penguin Group (USA) Inc., 375 Hudson Street, New York, New York 10014, U.S.A.
Penguin Books Ltd, 80 Strand, London WC2R 0RL, England
Penguin Ireland, 25 St Stephen's Green, Dublin 2, Ireland (a division of Penguin Books Ltd)
Penguin Group (Australia), 707 Collins Street, Melbourne, Victoria 3008, Australia
(a division of Pearson Australia Group Pty Ltd)
Penguin Books India Pvt Ltd, 11 Community Centre, Panchsheel Park, New Delhi – 110 017, India
Penguin Group (NZ), 67 Apollo Drive, Rosedale, Auckland 0632, New Zealand
(a division of Pearson New Zealand Ltd)
Penguin Books (South Africa) (Pty) Ltd, 24 Sturdee Avenue, Rosebank,Johannesburg 2196,
South Africa

Penguin Books Ltd, Registered Offices: 80 Strand, London WC2R 0RL, England

First published 2013

1 2 3 4 5 6 7 8 9 10

Manufactured in Canada

LIBRARY AND ARCHIVES CANADA CATALOGUING IN PUBLICATION

Stats Canada : satire on a national scale.

"From the experts behind the Twitter sensation @stats_canada"—Cover.

ISBN 978-0-14-318906-0 (pbk.)

1. National characteristics, Canadian—Humour. 2. Canada—Civilization—Humour. 3. Canada—
Statistics—Humour. 4. Satire, Canadian (English). 5. Twitter. 6. Title: @stats_canada (Twitter account)

FC173.S73 2013   971.07   C2013-905648-3

Visit the Penguin Canada website at **www.penguin.ca**

Special and corporate bulk purchase rates available; please see
www.penguin.ca/corporatesales or call 1-800-810-3104, ext. 2477.

Contents

For Becky

Introduction

A number of decades ago, we at Stats Canada came to the realization that we did not know much about the Canadian people. Sure, we knew about the increase in logging in British Columbia from 1987–1998, and about the number of unemployed children in the workforce (too many). However, we did not know about the Canadian people or their culture; about Canadian sports, dating in Canada, Canadian pop sensations, and what Canadians like to eat (donuts and Kraft Dinner, we came to find out).

In an attempt to learn more, Stats Canada has—through the magic of the federal taxation system—spent your hard-earned money to compile, sort, and analyze mounds of data on Canada and its people.

Through this process, we were able to ascertain some pretty interesting facts and recognize some shocking anomalies about this great nation. For example, did you know that more than 30% of Canadian Grade 5 students were not aware New

Brunswick even existed? Without our responsible, unbiased data collection we would never have known how little New Brunswick means to people.

Now, we at Stats Canada do realize that since we used your money to fund this investigation, we have a certain amount of responsibility to you. We demonstrate our commitment to this responsibility in three areas:

1. Stats Canada tries to keep costs down. For example, we ordered pizza only on Tuesdays (known as Pizza Tuesday—we made flyers). Also, instead of premium lager we brewed our own ale in our pal Ricky's bathtub.

2. Stats Canada maintains the highest possible standards in conducting our research. Therefore, we guarantee that only 15% of our findings came from Wikipedia. In addition, we hand-picked our population samples to ensure we chose the answers you would like the best.

3. Stats Canada recognizes our duty to share this research with you, the Canadian people (who paid for it). Hence, we've assembled all of our analyses and data into this fine publication, which you are free—nay, encouraged—

to purchase in multiple copies for yourself and your loved ones.

(Full disclosure: Proceeds from the sales of this book will go directly into the pockets of its authors. The money will be used to make future purchases of extravagant vacations, luxuriant fur coats, sexy red pants, and, of course, sparkling charm bracelets.)

Stats Canada hopes you gain as much insight and knowledge from reading this book as we have in the process of making it. *Si vous êtes en mesure de lire ceci, s'il vous plaît fermer le livre. Pas de Frenchies autorisés.* (Translation: If you are able to read this, please close the book. No Frenchies allowed.)

Stats Canada Census

1   Your Basic Information

Last Name: ☐☐☐☐☐☐☐☐☐☐☐☐☐☐☐☐

First Name: ☐☐☐☐☐☐☐☐☐☐ Middle Name: ☐☐☐☐☐☐☐☐☐☐

Twitter Handle: @☐☐☐☐☐☐☐☐☐

Fantasy Hockey Team Name: ☐☐☐☐☐☐☐☐☐☐

2   Your Address

What province or territory were you born in?

BC: ☐ Alberta: ☐ Saskatchewan: ☐ Manitoba: ☐ Ontario: ☐ Quebec: ☐ PEI: ☐

Nova Scotia: ☐ Newfoundland & Labrador: ☐ Yukon: ☐ NWT: ☐ Nunavut: ☐

What year did you move to Toronto? ☐☐☐☐ How long is your commute? ☐☐ hrs

How close is the nearest Mr. Sub? ☐☐☐ m Is it cold outside right now? Y̅N̅

3   Demographic Information

Favourite hockey team: | Leafs | Habs | Other |

Number of children over age 18 living at home: ☐

Number of snowblowers over age 18 stored in the garage: ☐

How many people in your household understand: English: ☐ French: ☐ 2-line passes: ☐

Number of folding camping chairs in your household: ☐☐☐

Do you play acoustic guitar at parties? Y̅N̅

Weight of change currently in your pockets: ☐☐☐ kg

Number of tattoos: ☐☐ Number of infected tattoos: ☐☐

On average, how much do you spend on healthcare per year? (just kidding)

Have you ever bought a mattress anywhere else: Y̅N̅

Favourite *Kids in the Hall* cast member:

4   Demographic Information (continued)

How many copies of *Jagged Little Pill* in your household:

Cassette: ☐   CD: ☐   Rhapsody.ca download: ☐

Please list the ages of all pairs of slippers in your household: ☐☐☐☐☐☐☐

Number of hours per week spent playing *Blades of Steel*:   ☐☐☐

Are you sexually attracted to your partner: Y☐N☐

Number of beer fridges in your household: ☐☐

Number of hand-me-down point blankets in your household: ☐☐

Number of hand-me-down point blankets in your cottage: ☐☐

Are they authentic: Y☐N☐

Favourite Mulroney: ☐ Brian ☐   ☐ Ben ☐

What's your dad's name: ☐ Gord ☐

How many Gords you have met this year: ☐☐☐☐

Would you consider naming a child Gord: Y☐N☐

Would you vote for a non-Gord prime minister: Y☐N☐

Have you ever broken a toonie into two pieces: Y☐N☐

Are you happy with your current financial institution: Y☐N☐

Are you into ghost towns: Y☐N☐

Would you buy an @stats_canada book: Y☐N☐

Do you remember the '90s: Y☐N☐

List three French curse words: ☐☐☐☐☐☐☐☐☐☐☐☐☐☐☐☐☐☐☐
☐☐☐☐☐☐☐☐☐☐☐☐☐☐☐☐☐☐☐
☐☐☐☐☐☐☐☐☐☐☐☐☐☐☐☐☐☐☐

List three Newfie jokes: ☐☐☐☐☐☐☐☐☐☐☐☐☐☐
☐☐☐☐☐☐☐☐☐☐☐☐☐☐
☐☐☐☐☐☐☐☐☐☐☐☐☐☐

☐☐☐☐☐☐☐☐☐☐☐☐☐☐
☐☐☐☐☐☐☐☐☐☐☐☐☐☐
☐☐☐☐☐☐☐☐☐☐☐☐☐☐

☐☐☐☐☐☐☐☐☐☐☐☐☐☐
☐☐☐☐☐☐☐☐☐☐☐☐☐☐
☐☐☐☐☐☐☐☐☐☐☐☐☐☐

Please connect with Facebook to complete this census

Canadian History

Early Canadian Stats

When the first European settlers set foot on Canadian soil, they struggled to make sense of the vast and hostile land before them. The British Crown quickly established *The Royal Council of Statistical Collection* in an attempt to understand and efficiently exploit their new and distant territory. In 1759, a battalion of bespectacled enumerators fanned out across British North America on a mission to record everything they encountered. A high rate of rabies infection rendered most of their findings incoherent, but from these primitive records a picture of Canada did begin to emerge. A bleak picture. Historians believe that Canada lay mostly uninhabited for many more decades because few homesteaders wanted to try their luck at settling a land so statistically unfriendly.

The findings of the first true Canadian census have languished forgotten in Stats Canada's basement. For the first time in more than two centuries, we present to you some key excerpts from the 1759 *Statistical Enumeration of Canadian Flora and Fauna*:

- Of the 7 animals I've seen today, 6 have bitten me
- 95% of the woodland berries in this forsaken land cause intractable diarrhea
- 1 in 10 of my toes appears to be dead
- 0% of the natives here know how to brew a cup of tea
- At least three types of plants here cause terrible irritation to exposed skin (esp. bottoms)
- 30% of my tears have frozen to my cheeks
- 100% of my canoes have floated away during the night
- Two-thirds of local mushrooms cause intractable diarrhea
- Wolf howls are 70% more scary at night

What Was the King–Byng Affair?

The King–Byng Affair marked a critical turning point in Canadian history, profoundly transforming the nature of the nation's government. Unfortunately, no living Canadian actually remembers what it was.

We asked ordinary Canadians what they thought the King–Byng Affair might be; these are the three most common answers:

- The controversy that erupted after King Clancy sold the Lady Byng Memorial Trophy to pay his bar tab
- The riots that devastated Vancouver after Nat King Cole and Bing Crosby's concert was cancelled in 1959
- Stephen Harper's failed attempt to make the Microsoft search engine the Official Search Engine of the Harper Government

While there's no way of knowing if any of the above are true, our data suggest that at least one of them probably is.

A Brief History of Smuggling

Canada has enjoyed a long-standing relationship with the United States. One of the benefits of this relationship is the ease of trade and commerce between nations. Some traded items are more popular than others, and some are more illegal than others. In this section we provide a brief history of the most popular illegal substances smuggled across the border.

Before the events of 0.818181,[1] bringing goods into the country was an entirely different affair. Clever Canadians could import goods up to $700 in value with just a smile and a wave. Offering a customs officer a cup of coffee was not yet seen as a potential act of terrorism.

Duty costs today are at an all-time high, even after accounting for Canadian inflation.[2] Compared to 1977, the requirement for

---

1 The metric system does not allow for fractions.
2 Based on Shoppers Optimum Points.

bringing a pair of jeans across the border has risen from a clever double-jeans-ing to a 15% surcharge and a 90-minute wait.

Duty Fees (1977)	
Cigarettes	1¢ per smoke
Beer	6¢ per stubby
Goldfish	3¢ per fin
Couches	25¢ per missing cushion

[*Editor's Note:* One time in the '80s, my dad was pulled over crossing into Canada, suspected of smuggling. Dad was adamant about the fact that his Ford Ranger contained no undeclared substances, but the customs agents persisted. After getting to the point of actually removing the seats from his truck, they found nothing illegal. They sent him on his way, but not before my father forced them to put his vehicle back together, because he had proven that he was not a liar. Long story short, they put his seats back the way they found them—which would never happen today.]

A Canadian History Timeline

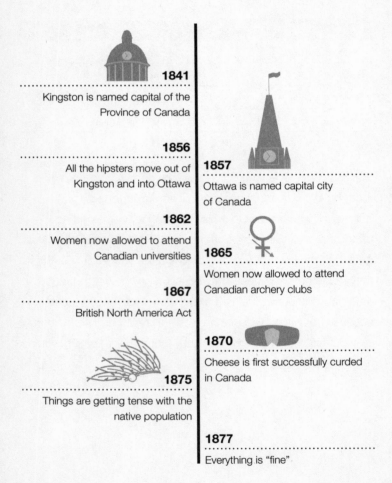

1841

Kingston is named capital of the Province of Canada

1856

All the hipsters move out of Kingston and into Ottawa

1857

Ottawa is named capital city of Canada

1862

Women now allowed to attend Canadian universities

1865

Women now allowed to attend Canadian archery clubs

1867

British North America Act

1870

Cheese is first successfully curded in Canada

1875

Things are getting tense with the native population

1877

Everything is "fine"

1885

First penny is flattened on the
Canadian Pacific Railway

1896

First "Cash 4 Gold" business is
started in the Klondike

1905

Salmon Arm, BC, is founded, mostly
as a joke

1910

The Newfie joke is invented

1919

Grandma is born

1924

New Brunswick is formed, probably

1939

Canada's buddy Nigel gets into a
fight with his neighbour

1945

They sort it out

1963

John Diefenbaker loses duel with
Lester B. Pearson

1967

Draft Dodger, Manitoba, is founded

1972

Savard passes to Henderson

1980 | **1980**

Sara is born | Tegan is born

1989

First "Heritage Minute" runs on television

1992

Blue Jays become first Canadian World Series championship team

1993

Blue Jays win again: Canadians try to learn the rules of baseball

1995

Bill C-68 guns something something

1998

Seinfeld series finale

2002

Canada finishes translating the Internet into French

Canada's Human Population vs. Bear Population

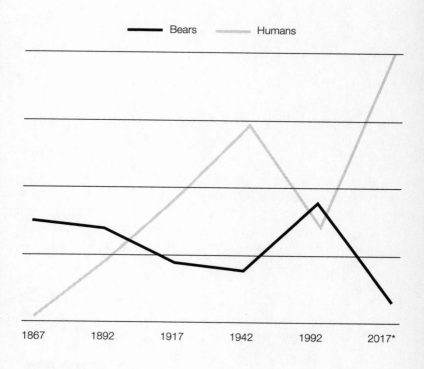

Bears — Humans

1867 1892 1917 1942 1992 2017*

*estimate

11

Canada's Population in Millions, 1867–2017

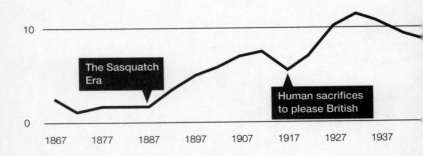

40 ─────────────────────────────

30 ─────────────────────────────

20 ─────────────────────────────

10 ─────────────────────────────

The Sasquatch Era

Human sacrifices to please British

0 ─────────────────────────────

1867   1877   1887   1897   1907   1917   1927   1937

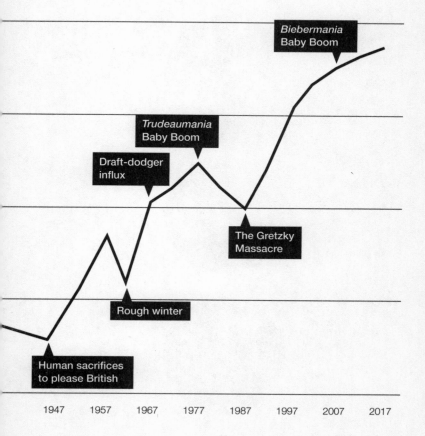

Biebermania
Baby Boom

Trudeaumania
Baby Boom

Draft-dodger
influx

The Gretzky
Massacre

Rough winter

Human sacrifices
to please British

1947 1957 1967 1977 1987 1997 2007 2017

Disposable Income Through History (Part One)

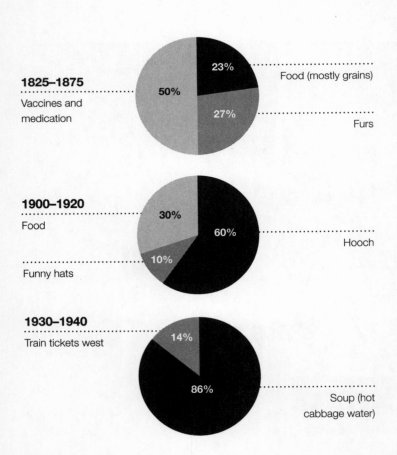

1825–1875

Vaccines and medication

50%

23% .... Food (mostly grains)

27% .... Furs

1900–1920

Food

30%

60% .... Hooch

10%

Funny hats

1930–1940

Train tickets west

14%

86% .... Soup (hot cabbage water)

Disposable Income Through History (Part Two)

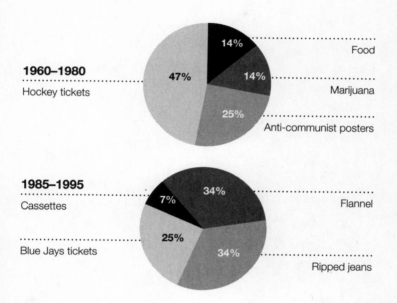

1960–1980
Hockey tickets

Food

Marijuana

Anti-communist posters

47%

14%

14%

25%

1985–1995
Cassettes

Blue Jays tickets

Flannel

Ripped jeans

34%

7%

25%

34%

Fathers of Confederation
Hockey Cards

GEORGE BROWN

Born: Scotland, 1818
Died: Toronto, 1880

A newspaperman before he was a politician, George Brown's Toronto paper *The Globe* denounced slavery in the American south and kicked off the Sudoku craze of the 1850s.

His "Clear Grit" party advocated for the separation of church and state and the annexation of Rupert's Land, and opposed the Keystone whale oil pipeline.

George Brown is perhaps best known for the Toronto College that bears his name, which is surprising because he was assassinated.

Number of colleges started	1
Favourite colour	Red
Power play goals	13
Secret crush	John A.
Number of times shot	1

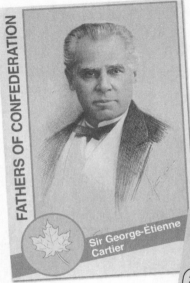

FATHERS OF CONFEDERATION

Sir George-Étienne Cartier

SIR GEORGE-ÉTIENNE CARTIER

Born: Quebec, 1814
Died: London, 1873

A dominant figure in the *Parti bleu* and the Premier of Canada East, Cartier was the Minister of Militia and Defence under Sir John A. Macdonald.

Cartier was largely responsible for bringing Quebec into confederation, a union that he engineered in exchange for a promise.

Known as somewhat of a rebel, Cartier was most often found wearing a cool leather jacket and smoking a hand-rolled cigarette.

Number of Lethbridges founded	0
Favourite brand of sheets	HBC
Assists	124
Secret crush	G.E. Cartier
Number of times shot	0

FATHERS OF CONFEDERATION

ALEXANDER TILLOCH GALT

ALEXANDER TILLOCH GALT

Born: England, 1817
Died: Montreal, 1893

Canada's first minister of finance, he both opposed and promoted trade with Britain and the United States at various points in his career—a fiscal policy he called "playing hard to get."

After a disagreement with John A. Macdonald over whose face would be on the ten-dollar bill, Galt left public service and founded the city of Lethbridge, Alberta, where he lived out his days as a conspicuously dandy cattle rancher.

Number of Lethbridges founded	1
Neckbeards	1
Penalty minutes	44
Secret crush	John A.
Number of times shot	0

James Cockburn

JAMES COCKBURN

Born: England, 1819
Died: Ottawa, 1883

Canada's first Speaker of the House, Cockburn, ironically, was not a man of his word. Despite being eleced as an opponent to the Macdonald-Cartier administration, Cockburn quickly crossed the floor and became a member of Macdonald's Liberal-Conservative party, which is why Benedict Arnold will forever be known as "The American James Cockburn."

Cockburn was known to spend long hours in the parliamentary library, where he quietly pursued his passion for Victorian erotica.

Parties belonged to	
Number of plaid vests	2
Boxers or briefs	4
Secret crush	Boxers
Number of times shot	John A.
	0

Laura Secord: Heroine, Positive Female Role Model, Chocolatier

According to a survey conducted in 2003, 88% of Canadian high school students believe that Laura Secord is a mythical creature. Stats Canada would like to educate the public with a trip back in time to take a look at Secord's triumphs.

Laura Secord is the third most important Canadian female role model after Kim Campbell, inventor of Campbell's soup, and Nellie McClung, who was the first Canadian woman to wear a pantsuit. Laura was the eldest daughter of Thomas Ingersoll and Elizabeth Dewey, born on September 13, 1775, in Barrington, Massachusetts. (So, you know, not Canadian. Minor detail.)

Secord, a renowned chocolatier, had been supplying nearby Mousse, Upper Canada, with her famed chocolates for years. On the evening of June 21, 1813, during the War of 1812, Laura Secord was catering to a group of American soldiers who had forced their way into her home for an evening snack. Once the soldiers were three sheets to the wind they revealed their plans to invade and open a chocolate factory as well as their own chain of chocolate stores in Mousse.

This could not stand! I mean, everybody loved Laura's selection of fine, handcrafted chocolates and this whole big plan would totally hurt business. How could she compete? Oh, and yeah, there was the whole invasion idea ... but seriously, the chocolate business was HER THING.

Laura Secord selflessly began her pilgrimage to Mousse early the next morning in the cruel heat of June. "I'm sorry, it's like they've never even tried my French and Frosted Mint," Laura thought to herself. "YEAH, DELICIOUS, I know. What do they have? Chocolate and peanut butter or something? Yeah, REAL sophisticated, guys. Americans, eh?" Laura was really sensitive about the possible invasion, like, almost too sensitive about it, but whatever.

Okay, right. So, Laura left for Mousse to warn everyone that there was a really UNcool American company coming to town and it was going to "take away from the local mom-and-pop businesses" and "invade or whatever! Who cares! I'm going to go broke!" She successfully made it to her destination and was able to warn the people of Mousse—who were grateful, but at the same time it was bittersweet (chocolate joke) because they were kind of curious as to what the Yankees had in store.

Laura was so darned proud of herself, she commemorated her plight by putting her own face on one of her chocolates.

Which everyone thought was a bit much, but were too scared to tell her.

Prime Ministers Yearbook

John A. Macdonald
Class of 1891
Clubs: Chess Club (founding member), Sailing
Club (founding member), School Prime Minister,
Model Train Club (founding member)
Future Plans: To get wasted!!!! YOLO!!!!
Voted Nicest Eyes

Wilfrid Laurier
Class of 1911
Clubs: 4H Club, Mathletes, Improv Club
Future Plans: Move to the new province of
Saskatchewan, the land of opportunity

Arthur Meighen

Class of 1926
Clubs: None
Sports: None
Future Plans: None
Quote: "I won't be forgotten if they name a small, uninhabitable island in the Arctic Ocean after me, right? ... right?"

William Lyon Mackenzie King

Class of 1926
Clubs: Ouija Board Club, Taxidermy Club, Barbershop Quartet
Future Plans: Continue living with my mother
Quote: "Let sleeping dogs lie and dead ones listen to all your problems."

Pierre Trudeau

Class of 1984
Clubs: Model UN, President of the Presidents Club, Newspaper editor, Modern Dance Team, Voted Most Likely to Become a Sex Symbol for Reasons Unknown to Us

Brian Mulroney

Class of 1993
Clubs: French Club, Toastmasters, President
of the Jay Leno Fan Club
Quote: "I hope my son uses hair gel correctly."

Kim Campbell

Class of 1993
Clubs: Future Homemakers of Canada
Sports: Track and Field (district record for fastest
time on a short track)
Quote: "Girls can do anything guys can do, but
only for four months."

Jean Chrétien

Class of 2003
Sports: Boxing, Tae Kwan Do, Muay Thai,
Women's Self-Defence, Wrestling, Karate
Awards: Spelling Bee Champion
Quote: "Ehhhhh, I see da fut-cher as full of ...
ehhhh ... oppor-ehhhh-tunity and unity."

Culture AND Language

Language in Canada

Like the glorious maple tree, whose leaves explode in a kaleidoscope of colour every autumn, Canadians from coast to coast to coast speak with a dizzying palette of languages and accents. From the unintelligibly mush-mouthed dialect of the Avalon Peninsula to Vancouver Island's laconic platitudes, Canadian tongues do a lot of work when they're not stuck to a metal pole.

Canadian English

Canadian English is like Canadian culture itself, starting out with a distinct British influence but corrupted over years of close contact with Americans. On paper, Canadian English has retained most of its British heritage, decorating itself with the charming *u* and eschewing the vulgar *s* for the occasional exotic *z*. To foreign ears, however, Canadians are often indistinguishable from Americans. This common misunderstanding has spawned the two-billion-loonie backpack flag industry.

Pronunciation

Although Canadians struggle to hear it with their own ears, Canadian speakers are most easily identified by the way they raise certain vowels. It is this tendency, caused by maple syrup residue on the tongue, that has led to the familiar "aboot" stereotype. Many a Canadian in a foreign land has been ooted this way.

Bilingualism

English and French both enjoy official status in Canada, guaranteeing that the government, private sector, and cereal boxes all conduct themselves in both languages. Although English speakers outnumber French speakers 4:1, the powerful Quebec cheese lobby has wielded a startling amount of parliamentary power, manipulating the national appetite for curds to guarantee Canada remains officially bilingual.

French Education

Nearly all English Canadians study some French in elementary school, 75% of which consists of memorizing out-of-context verb conjugations. The most-owned and least-read book in Canada is the *Bescherelle*. For many English Canadians, the first French speaker they meet is "Ananas," the playful pineapple puppet and star of a series of educational videos that have forever associated francophone culture with tropical fruit.

Quebec

Among the 10 Canadian provinces, Quebec is the only one whose majority are francophones, although significant but *très petite* French-speaking communities can be found in Ontario, Manitoba, and New Brunswick. If French Canadians were distributed evenly across the nation, it has been calculated that Roch Voisine would be a lot more popular outside of Quebec. Language is a hot-button issue in Quebec, where local laws require that all signs, product packaging, and tattoos display French words more prominently than English ones. The French spoken throughout Canada differs significantly from what you might hear in a Parisian café, and many outsiders have a hard time making sense of the local *joual*. It's no wonder that Quebec's only significant cultural export, *Just for Laughs: Gags*, relies on the universal language of pranks and pratfalls.

Most Frequently Used *Joual* Expressions	
Le hot-dog	A sausage-like meat, served on a bun
Le weekend	A two-day rest period at the end of the week
Han?!	Eh? Huh? What?
Eniway	In any case, anyway
Ouuuuuuuais	Yeah, yep

Other Languages

Our recent census results tell us that an increasing number of Canadians are speaking a language other than English or French at home, reflecting the changing face of Canadian culture. In rec rooms across the nation, Canadians can be heard swearing at televised hockey games in Punjabi, Italian, Mandarin, Portuguese, and Tagalog. Many of these communities have adapted to their new homeland by finding new words to describe the country and culture surrounding them. There is now a Malay word for double-double, and an Arabic expression to describe damp socks.

Regional Dialects

Among the 28 million Canadians who are fluent in English, regional differences abound. The largest diversity occurs in Atlantic Canada, where nearly every Maritime fishing cove seems to have its own local dialect. The English spoken here contains so many local expressions and idioms that most words are abandoned almost as soon as they're spoken. They call this "catch and release."

In Southern Ontario, Canadians sound a bit like their American neighbours, a phenomenon that dates back to the pre-0.818181[1]

---

1 See footnote 1 on page 6.

years, when cross-border shopping was easier and the dialect snuck over the border along with undeclared milk and cheap jeans from J.C. Penney.

Northwest of the Great Lakes, the Canadian language takes on a different flavour. In this endless land of bush and pothole lakes, the long winters and short summer seasons have led to a culture of casual conservation. The locals save precious energy by dropping as many phonetic sounds as possible, and by letting their Polaris snowmobile jackets do the talking.

Across the prairies, the Ukrainian, Scandinavian, and German settlers who first broke the land also sowed the area with a linguistic legacy. Their speech patterns persist in the local language like the stink of potato stew. It is also here where you'll hear a hoodie called a "bunny hug," underpants a "gotch," and persistent knife violence a "fact of life."

On the Pacific coast, the English spoken in British Columbia is the least recognizably Canadian of all local dialects. Canadian speech patterns can't scale the imposing Rocky Mountains, allowing Seattle's bland accent to settle upon the region like a fog.

The Future

All language is in a constant state of flux, but our surveys suggest that many uniquely Canadian idioms and speech patterns will persist. Canadian language is evolving with the times, with many Canadianisms migrating to the digital world as easily textable abbreviations:

Dx2: "double-double"

MOTH: "moose on the highway"

LOLS: "long Oilers losing streak"

(o Y o): "there's an owl watching me"

24424: "don't forget to pick up a case of beer for Victoria Day weekend"

YOLO: "YOLO"

The Canadian Dictionary

While gathering data on Canadian culture, Stats Canada began to notice that Canadians use several words unique to Canada. Given the importance of language to a unified culture, we have determined the top five most Canadian words:

poutine \ POO-teen \ *noun*
1 the official food of Quebec, made of french fries, gravy, and cheese curds; consumed on a daily basis by the majority of Quebecois.

Examples
"Hey, Henri, do you want to go get some poutine before we have a conversation entirely in French because we live in Quebec?"

"This poutine is delicious, Jacques. I especially like the cheese curds because I am French and we French love cheese more than anything."

Did You Know?

Quebecois chef Pierre Peugeot experimented with adding cheese curds and gravy to many different foods before stumbling upon french fries. Some of the failed versions of poutine included Shreddies, sliced bananas, frogs' legs, crêpes, and other types of cheese.

- -

loonie \ lu:ni \ *noun*

1 the Canadian one-dollar coin.

2 a measurement of the strength of the Canadian currency.

Examples

"Can I borrow a loonie from you, Becky? I need to buy a chocolate bar from the convenience store."

"The loonie is up 4% today on the international market, eh Gord?"

Did You Know?

The Canadian one-dollar coin was introduced in 1987 and replaced the one-dollar bill. Before the coin was minted the Canadian government allowed the people to decide what would appear on its reverse side. The iconic loon won with 57% of the votes cast. However, some of the other popular votes were:

Wayne Gretzky ("the Gretzkie") – 19%
Anne of Green Gables ("the Annie") – 5%
Winnie-the-Pooh ("the Poohie") – 5%
A polite, apologetic wave ("the Sorrie") – 4%
Misc. write-in votes – 1%

. . . .

bud \ 'bəd \ *noun*
1 a form of chummy address, usually to a boy or man, used primarily when greeting a fellow Canadian or just before a fight breaks out.

Examples
"Did ya see the Leafs lose the game last night, bud? It was a real blowout, eh?"

"Say that to my face, bud!"

Did You Know?
The familiar greeting "bro" is the American equivalent of "bud." Whereas "bro" is mostly used by fraternity brothers and surf

bums, "bud" has more widespread and common usage. In fact, 71% of Canadians will refer to one another as "bud" while conversing, and the term is acceptable in business relationships and legal proceedings.

- -

tuque \ too-K \ *noun*
1 a winter/all-year hat in Canada, typically made from lambswool or a beaver pelt.

Examples

"Johnny, it is minus 48 out there today, eh? Make sure you wear at least three tuques."

"Nice tuque, bud! Did you get that from a Molson 2-4?"

Did You Know?

In Canada, the tuque is the number-one-selling article of clothing, more popular than underwear, t-shirts, or jeans. The tuque was responsible for 61% of all retail clothing sales in 2011. That number of course does not include hand-knit tuques from your grandmother, which are the nation's second most popular Christmas gift—surpassed only by copies of *The Hockey Sweater* by Roch Carrier.

chirp \ (trp) \ *verb*

1 to insult another Canadian, with a focus on sexual or hockey team preference.

Examples

"Coach, I had to throw my gloves off, they were chirpin' me. They said my mom was overweight."

"Don't chirp me, bud."

Did You Know?

Chirping originated in rural Saskatoon when a group of birds pestered an outdoor junior hockey game. Every missed pass or flubbed save garnered a bevy of chirps from the hovering flock. The term "chirp" came to describe the practice of insulting young hockey players, and later was adapted to cover general insults amongst Canadians.

Top Canadian Pastimes

According to a survey conducted by Stats Canada in 2007, the top 20 Canadian pastimes are as follows:

- Cooking bacon
- Eating bacon
- Practising loon calls
- Practising loon whispering
- Reading old copies of *HELLO! Canada* at the salon
- Not complaining
- Holding doors open
- Tobogganing (drunk)
- Tobogganing (sober)
- Shovelling snow for neighbours
- Talking to neighbours about shovelling snow
- Waiting for tea to steep

- Being polite and courteous

- Considering snow tires

- Counting Canadian Tire money

- Throwing away Canadian Tire money

- Filling up the beer fridge

- Opening the cottage

- Picking fights with other parents in the stands during house league hockey games

- Chirping Vancouver Canucks fans via tweet

 Did You Know?

79% of Canadians just mouth the words during the French part of the national anthem.

What Do Canadians Learn in School?

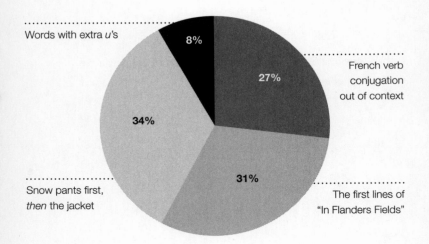

Words with extra *u*'s

8%

27%

French verb
conjugation
out of context

34%

31%

Snow pants first,
then the jacket

The first lines of
"In Flanders Fields"

Education and the Workforce

As of 2009, 49% of Canadians aged 25 to 64 have some form of post-secondary education. This means that 49% of Canadian Tire employees are falling far short of their dreams. Statistically, Canadians is a smart people, but they must adapt to the changing economic climate. Today's young Canadians have completely different job prospects than their parents:

Old Job	New Job
Welder	Waiter
Farmer	Barista
Butcher	Tattoo Artist
Machinist	Apple Store Genius
Journalist	Paperboy
Lawyer	YouTube Commenter
Seamstress	American Apparel Cashier
Don Cherry	Don Cherry
Secretary	iPhone Memo App
Banker	Kickstarter
Homeowner	Slumlord
Nerd	Millionaire Bachelor

Classroom hours spent during elementary school education
(all years):

- 440 hours learning cursive writing
- 1,600 hours learning the *passé composé*
- 2,000 hours learning metric multiplication tables
- 850 hours playing Crosscountry Canada
- 1,250 hours playing ringette

Compared to developed nations with similar climates and schoolbus commutes, Canada has become 25% less educationally competitive and 35% less excited about picture day.

The outlook is not all bleak. Some school boards are embracing the modern workplace by encouraging students to tweet their homework and "poke" their teachers. Drama class has given way to Facebook drama class, and out-of-date textbooks have been replaced with first-generation iPads.

These futile grasps at educational reform are ultimately trivial, however, compared to the nation's official long-term strategy for recovering its competitive advantage: importing smart foreigners. Every day, planeloads of clever and motivated youngsters are absorbed into school systems nationwide. Their young minds, untainted by exposure to fatty breakfast meats and numbing episodes of *Just for Laughs: Gags*, will power the nation to prosperity. Canada's history of welcoming newcomers will pay off as their precious brains are woven into the cultural mosaic. Take that, Finland.

Did You Know?

Canada is 50% the letter A.

How Do Canadians
Spend Their Workday?

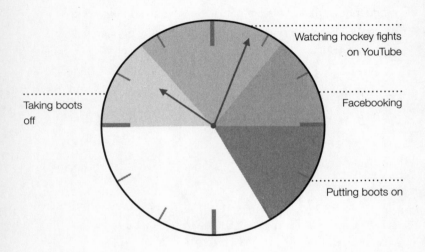

Watching hockey fights
on YouTube

Facebooking

Putting boots on

Taking boots

How Do Retirees
Spend Their Time?

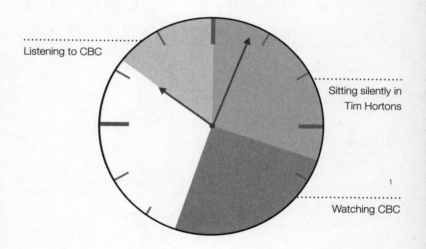

Listening to CBC

Sitting silently in
Tim Hortons

Watching CBC

Top Manufactured Goods by Province

Province	Top Manufactured Good
Ontario	Leafs Tickets
Newfoundland and Labrador	Worm Traps
Nova Scotia	Cool Hats
PEI	Television Icons
Quebec	Cool Breads
British Columbia	Slacklines
Yukon	Trinkets Carved from Bone
Saskatchewan	Gluten
Northwest Territories	Licence Plates
Manitoba	Unsolved Mysteries
Nunavut	Strange Leathery Goods
New Brunswick	[More Data Required]
Alberta	Barrels

How Do Canadians Get to Work?

Mode of Transportation	Number of Canadians Using It (in Millions)
Car	12.6
Subway	2.8
Ferry	1.2
Snowmobile	4.7
Dog Sled	5.1
Cross-Country Skis	4.9
Chad Kroeger	1.8
Ice Skates	4.1
Walking	0.07

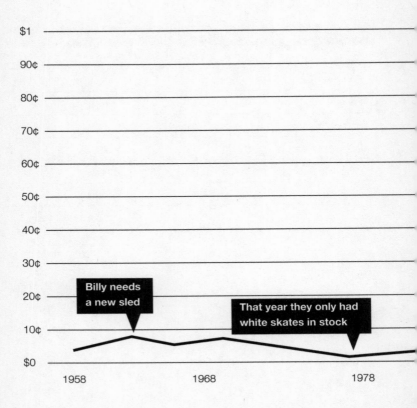

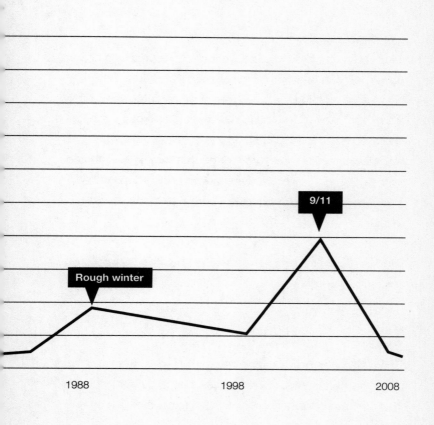

Rough winter

9/11

1988   1998   2008

Female Beavers in Canada: A Gender-Based Statistical Report

Life Expectancy

Female beavers make up just over half of the Canadian beaver population with 52.6%, which has been a very close majority held for the past four decades; this number represents roughly 2.2 million beavers. The quality of life for female beavers has improved and beavers in general are experiencing lower mortality rates. Less demand for pelts has directly contributed to the rise in population, a phenomenon not seen since the Raccoon Boom following the 1884 downfall of the coonskin cap industry.

Studies project that the female beaver population will continue to maintain a slight majority over male beavers for the next 70 years.

Family

The majority of mature female beavers are in a committed domestic partnership. Overall, female beavers are still maintaining a traditional position in the family. The average colony consists of a monogamous, heterosexual pair heading the family and 9.7 children.

Female-headed single-beaver homes have reached 23%, an all-time high that has been steadily increasing since the early 1990s. Same-sex dam-holds are on the rise but still continue to represent only 4% of colonies.

Colonies are experiencing "empty lodge syndrome" at a slower rate than in the past. Traditionally, at the age of maturity (two years) beavers leave the dam to either learn a trade or start their own colony. Since the early 2000s, the number of mature beavers living at home has increased. It is notable that 46% of female beavers with a mature beaver still living at home maintain a full-time job.

Education

The literacy rate for female beavers is 0%, while 100% are fluent in a language known as "tail talk": beavers use their large waffle tails to tap out a series of signals similar to Morse code.

The most popular fields of study for beavers are trades in relation to wood, dental hygiene, and the pulp and paper industry.

Conclusion

Current trends suggest that female beavers are living longer, more prosperous lives. Female beavers are filling jobs that would traditionally be held by male beavers and are working and raising a colony simultaneously. With the exception of pay inequality, female beavers are breaking barriers and assuming greater responsibilities than their ancestors.

Did You Know?

The minimum wage in Canada is 9 compliments per hour.

Top Canadian Baby Names

Male	Female
Gord	Alanis
Kim	Kim
Bob	Céline
Doug	Sharon
Bram	Lois
Zamboni	Becky
John	Tegan
Jean	Sara
Jian	Luba
Chad	Avril
Drake	Nelly

Birth and Death Rates

An average of 12,000 babies are born in Canada every year; each one of them is kissed on the forehead by the Queen. Since the divorce rate in Canada is only 13% (due to couples needing each other's body warmth to survive the harsh winter), babies tend to be born into two-parent families.

Most women carry babies for 11 to 12 months, for no other reason than that it's so dang warm and cozy in there! The average family will have 5 kids, or enough to have an entire team for shinny.

Canadian babies are born with the ability to fish, hunt, and gather. Up until the 21st century it was commonplace for women to give birth in the wilderness; if the baby then found its way back to society, it was accepted into the family. Some less successful "wilderness babies" still remain throughout the Rocky Mountains and on the Gaspé Peninsula.

Children are fitted for hockey skates at 9 months, once weight can be placed on the feet. At 4 years they are tested in agility, strength, and how fast their slapshot is. If they meet certain criteria, they are placed in community hockey leagues. The failures usually become actors on *Degrassi* or members of parliament.

Since Canada is one of the top places to live in the world, male citizens tend to live to the average age of 96, while women, such as Anne Murray, will never die.

Old people not only comprise the entire viewership for the CBC, but also are used by the Canadian Armed Forces to bore the nation's enemies into just going away. The most popular stories told are (1) "Why I have that dead toe"; (2) "Why I have that other dead toe"; and (3) "Back in my day, The Bay put 5 stripes on their blankets."

In 2012, the population of Canada grew by 4.7%, factoring in the birth and death rate as well as stupid Americans trying to dodge the draft, Russian brides, and members of the Winnipeg Jets.

What Can Canadians Buy with Their Shoppers Optimum Points?

Point Amount	Reward
8,000	Nothing
22,000	A comb
38,000	A one-year subscription to *Chatelaine*
50,000	A lead role on CBC's *Republic of Doyle*
95,000	A one-way Via Rail ticket to Windsor, Ontario

How Canadians Die

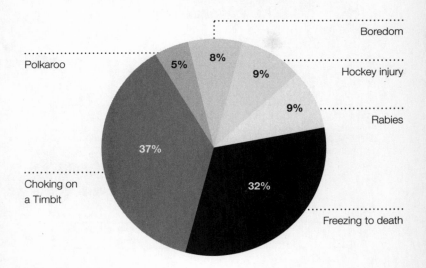

Boredom 8%

Hockey injury 9%

Rabies 9%

Freezing to death 32%

Choking on a Timbit 37%

Polkaroo 5%

How Canadian Are You?

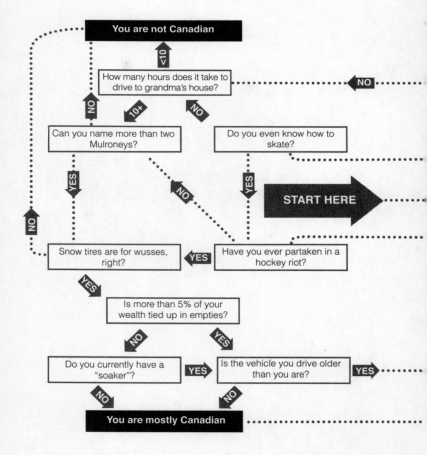

You are not Canadian

<10

How many hours does it take to drive to grandma's house? — NO

10+   NO

Can you name more than two Mulroneys?

Do you even know how to skate?

NO

YES   YES

START HERE

Snow tires are for wusses, right? — YES — Have you ever partaken in a hockey riot?

NO

YES

Is more than 5% of your wealth tied up in empties?

NO   YES

Do you currently have a "soaker"? — YES — Is the vehicle you drive older than you are? — YES

NO   NO

You are mostly Canadian

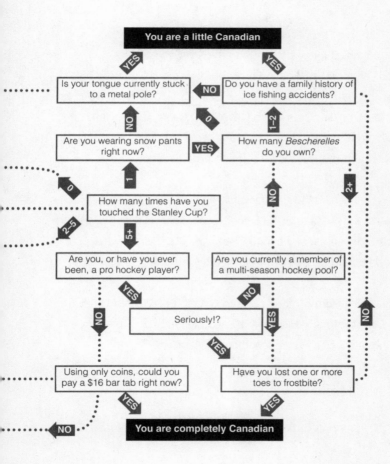

You are a little Canadian

YES → Is your tongue currently stuck to a metal pole?

YES → Do you have a family history of ice fishing accidents?

NO (between the two top boxes)

NO ↓ Is your tongue currently stuck to a metal pole?

Are you wearing snow pants right now?

YES → How many *Bescherelles* do you own?

0 → Do you have a family history of ice fishing accidents?

1-2 → Do you have a family history of ice fishing accidents?

1 ↑ Are you wearing snow pants right now?

How many times have you touched the Stanley Cup?

0 →

2-5 →

5+ ↓

NO ↓ How many *Bescherelles* do you own?

2+ ↓

Are you, or have you ever been, a pro hockey player?

Are you currently a member of a multi-season hockey pool?

NO ↓

YES → Seriously!?

NO → Are you currently a member of a multi-season hockey pool?

YES ↓

NO ↑

YES →

Using only coins, could you pay a $16 bar tab right now?

Have you lost one or more toes to frostbite?

YES ↓

YES ←

NO ←

You are completely Canadian

Stamps Canada

Since the first letter exchanged hands via dogsled team in 1527, stamps have played an important role in Canada's history. The first Canadian stamp was actually a practical joke, when a nobleman glued a sixpence to a letter, making it difficult for the mailman to collect. The trend caught on much to the chagrin of Canada Post, then known as Glen & Horse Co.

Stamps have shaped the development of Canada. New Brunswick speaks mostly French because the English-speaking mailmen went on strike for a week in 1890. Every Canadian now has to spend at least one year of duty with the postal service.

The British North America Stamp Act of 1850 decreed that all stamps are protected historical documents and cannot be desecrated, burned, or licked by peasants.

Stamp Facts

- The glue on the back of Canadian stamps is organic tree sap mixed with local moose spit. The exact formula is a guarded secret, known only to those who ask nicely.

- The back of each stamp is the same stamp, but in French.

- Handwritten letters are still quite popular in Canada because too many emails will shut down the Internet in the Atlantic provinces.

The most valuable Canadian stamp is a depiction of the Queen, where a printing defect makes it look like there is a polyp on the young Queen's face. Polyp Queen is well known in the stamp collector world, even though the whole thing is inherently gross. A small batch circulated in 1960 before being discontinued; the Royal Family took great offence to this and declined to visit Canada for 30 years after the incident. During this era of very little British influence, Canada held two Olympic games, passed the Charter of Rights and Freedoms, and created *Degrassi Junior High*. All of these events were later commemorated in stamp form.

Lesser-Known Canadian Stamps

- Shirtless Gordie Howe
- The Queen's Best Friend Ian
- Sleep Country Canada
- Giant Tiger Bicentennial
- Soups of Canada
- The Elderly of Saskatoon
- Anti-Australia Propaganda
- Weird Birds of Canada
- Maple Glazed
- The Fedoras of Scarborough
- Salmon Arm
- Shawinigan Handshake (or, That Time Jean Chrétien Chokeslammed a Protester)

Niceness

Everyone says that Canadians are the nicest people in the world, but we here at Stats Canada don't believe everything we hear. What follows is a statistical analysis of just how nice Canadians are.

Let's start with a simple example. Canada is the leading country in the world for holding the door open for ladies/elderly ladies. Modern women are indeed doin' it for themselves, but statistically very few Canadians will turn down a kind gesture. Here, we break it down per capita:

- Toronto: 9.5 million doors held open vs. 4 million independent ladies
- Calgary: 3.0 million doors held open vs. 1.1 million lonely prairie roses
- Halifax: 1.9 million doors held open vs. 900,000 fishermen's wives

Compare this to such non-Canadian cities as:

- Detroit: 1.7 million doors held open vs. 3.9 million seniors getting groceries
- Miami: 3.2 million doors held open vs. 8 million strong Latina women who hold their own doors open

Canada is also a world leader in interacting with strangers. Statistics show that Canadians will receive an average of 3.4 unsolicited greetings during their morning commute alone.[1] These interactions may include an affable wave from an elderly man, someone giving up their seat on the bus, or a nice young man rescuing you and your dog from a burning building.

Further examples of nice things Canadians do:

- Refrain from making fun of each other's tuques
- Wait patiently for proper healthcare
- Acknowledge their shortcomings within the genre of rap music
- Let American teams win the Stanley Cup
- Serve as totally chill customs agents

---

1 Please note this dataset does not include Torontonians, as they are a cold and distant people.

The statistics gathered do not reflect only human activity. In fact, our research has revealed acts of kindness committed by the country itself. For example:

- Keeping America's head warm
- Having a built-in shield
- Breaking up fights between the oceans
- Providing a safe haven for the French
- Sharing Bieber

Did You Know?

The average Canadian weighs 0.7 Americans.

Canadians and Free Healthcare

One of the many things Canada is known for is its free
healthcare. If Canadians break a leg or contract a hockey-
equipment-related rash, they need not pay to be seen by a
doctor. Instead the doctor is paid for by Canadians' taxes.
This is a point of pride for many Canadians and contributes
significantly to Canada being better than the United States.
However, free healthcare is not all good. Unfortunately, when

Reason for Visit to the Doctor	American Wait Times	American Treatment Cost
Common Cold	15 minutes	$1,300
Broken Bone	2 minutes	$12,900
Breast Implants	Walk-in service	$15,000/breast
Invasive Surgery	10 minutes (for processing)	Your first-born child or one of your left appendages

something is free it loses its value. The average Canadian is 15 times more likely to go see a doctor for a runny nose or itchy eyes than the average American, which of course drives up wait times to see a physician.

Even given the extended wait times, 97% of Canadians would still rather wait to be seen by a doctor than pay for the service. To further complicate matters, healthcare systems do exist that have lower wait times and are still free. However, when asked, only 9% of Canadians would be willing to actually move to Europe, even though they have better healthcare. Europe is just that bad.

Canadian Wait Times	Canadian Treatment Cost
2 days, 13 hours	Free (possibly $5 for antibiotics)
14 hours	Free (compliment the family photo on the doctor's desk and you'll receive a premium cast signed by members of your favourite hockey team)
Drive time to USA	$15,000/breast
2–3 weeks	Free (the secet handshake will upgrade you to the hospital's luxury OR and recovery room)

Top Five Ailments Afflicting Canadians

1. The Sniffles
2. Salmon Arm
3. Smugness (Toronto and Vancouver)
4. L'Estomac du fromage (Quebec and New Brunswick)
5. Bieber Fever

What's That Smell?

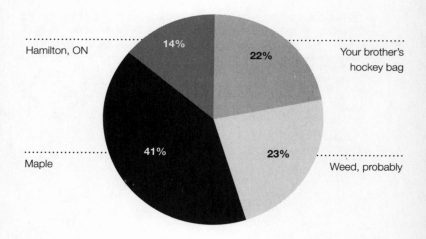

Hamilton, ON — 14%

Your brother's hockey bag — 22%

Maple — 41%

Weed, probably — 23%

Notable Canadian Inventions

Invention	Invented By
Mittens	Marc Garneau, first Canadian in space
Abdominal Muscles	Ryan Gosling
Time Travel	Sir Sandford Fleming
Basketball	Steve Nash
Irony	Alanis Morissette
Ben Mulroney	Brian Mulroney

Canadian Inventions:
Important vs. Not Important

Invention	Important	Not Important
Canadarm	√	
Kerosene	√	
Snowmobile		√
IMAX		√
Electron Microscope	√	
Electronic Organ		√
Insulin	√	
SONAR	√	
Basketball		√
Ice Hockey	√	
Butter Tarts	√	
Garbage Bags	√	

Wildlife Profile:
The Red Olympic Mitten

Kingdom: Accessoria

Class: Knittia

Order: Made in China

Family: Olympia

Genus: Patriotism

Distribution of the Red Olympic Mitten

Distribution

The Red Olympic Mitten can be found only in Canada and thrives in every region despite the varying temperatures.

Breeding

This species was bred specifically for the 2010 Vancouver Olympic Games and production has ceased. Normally this would render a species endangered; however, because of the durability of the Red Olympic Mitten, the population is far from dying out.

Much like the beaver, the Red Olympic Mitten is monogamous and will mate for life. When separated from its partner the mittens are subject to a solitary existence lying bereft on Canadian sidewalks, jammed into shopping mall escalators, or languishing in elementary school lost and found bins.

Description

The Red Olympic Mitten has a knitted, bloated exterior. One mitten is large enough to fit a family of small rabbits or one medium-sized rodent. The white markings on the underside of the Red Olympic Mitten

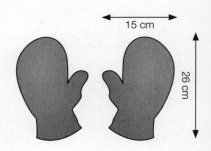

15 cm

26 cm

represent a maple leaf; on the other side, Vancouver 2010.

Diet

The Red Olympic Mitten survives solely on spilled coffee and maple dip donut crumbs.

22 Ways to Break a Toonie

- Hammer

- Asking politely

- Leaving it in the freezer

- Biting it

- Melting it

- Drowning it

- Stern words

- Hitting it with another toonie

- Shame

- Using it as a pog slammer

- Running over it with a train

- Mini-sticks

- Prolonged inflation

- High-fiving it in front of a loonie

- Challenging it to a drinking game

- Summoning the polar bear gods

- Pleading

- Bargaining

- Thinking positive thoughts

- Befriending a loonie to make it jealous

- Dropping it from a tall, free-standing structure

- One loonie, three quarters, one dime, one nickel, ten pennies

 Did You Know?

The average Canadian says sorry over 45,000 times a day.

Is It Canadian or American?

	American	Canadian
Condiment	Ranch	Ketchup
Carbonated Beverage	Soda	Pop
Chips	Chocolate	Ketchup
Comedy	Jeff Foxworthy	Brent Butt
Coffee	Soda	Double-double

Biggest Differences Between Canada and the USA

Canada

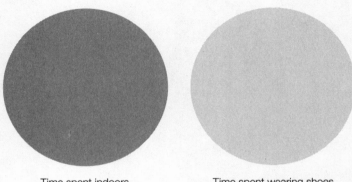

Time spent indoors   Time spent wearing shoes

USA

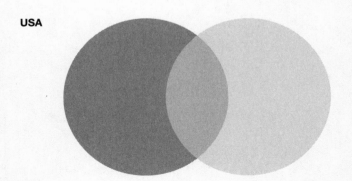

How Do Canadians Use Ice?

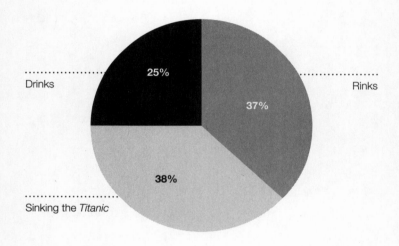

Drinks 25%

Rinks 37%

Sinking the *Titanic* 38%

Geography AND Regions

The Geography of Canada

At 9,970,610 square kilometres, Canada is one of the largest countries in the world. The vast area of Canadian land includes a diverse array of geographical zones, from the mountains in the west, to the tundra in the north, to the tundra in the east, and the tundra in the south.

93% of Canada is surrounded by water. This is why Canadians are known as such excellent water athletes.[1] In fact, 1 in 10 Canadian commuters get to work by swimming—a task made more difficult by the sub-zero temperatures.

The varying geographical regions of Canada dictate the types of shelters Canadians live in. In the Rocky Mountains 97% of the population are black bears, who typically like to live in alpine caves. These caves are furnished with items from the local IKEA

---

1 The most popular collegiate sport in Canada is water polo, which is played by the vast majority of fraternity brothers (commonly known as "bros").

and usually have many affordable throw rugs to provide warmth from the cold rock floor.

On the east coast many of the residents are fishermen, meaning they prefer to live on the sea. Houseboats are the most popular form of shelter; about 79% of the local population live in floating homes.

The prairies are the flattest part of Canada and provide little shelter from the elements. The winds in Saskatchewan have been measured at 110 km/h and 93 degrees below zero (Celsius). The weather is so harsh in the prairies that most of the population has migrated underground where the wind will not bother them. Saskatoon, Saskatchewan, is the largest (both in population and in land mass) entirely subterranean metropolis in the world.

The Trans-Canada Highway

Eight megametres long and clearly visible from space, the Trans-Canada Highway is Canada's most famous landmark. A Niagara of tar and gravel, this serpentine band of Canadian ingenuity traces a storied route across an epic landscape. Like China's Great Wall, or Mexico's Panama Canal, Canada's greatest accomplishment in civil engineering has become a symbol of the country itself.

It's hard to fully comprehend the massive scale of Canada's most important road. More than two-thirds of Alberta's tar sands industry is devoted to resurfacing the highway each spring. The average Canadian travels the equivalent of its entire length about six times every year. If it were laid out end to end, the Trans-Canada Highway would actually extend from one side of the country to the other. Fondly called the "TCH" by the hundreds who use it every day, few things loom larger in the Canadian consciousness than this truly magnificent road.

Early Canadians long dreamed of conquering the nation's inhospitable terrain, but efforts to plot a land route between "Lower Canada" and "Roughrider Country" proved difficult. Canada's young history was built on the backs of sturdy men who mushed across the muskeg on dogsleds or paddled silently along the nation's many waterways. Some tried to carve out permanent passages through the wilderness, but the thick boreal forest quickly swallowed up any progress behind them. Few returned.

The total absence of roads in pre-Confederation Canada proved fortuitous when, in 1812, American aggressors crossed the 49th parallel in search of a fight. Their progress was quickly thwarted when their supply wagons became hopelessly stuck in the mossy Canadian earth.

Highway scholars consider Canada's early-20th-century "ice roads" to be the prototype for what would eventually become the Trans-Canada Highway. Travel on these icy roads was often slow because of the many shinny games one was likely to encounter along the way.

With the advent of the automobile and the influence of American popular culture seeping over the border, Canadians longed for a chance to cruise on their very own stretch of pavement. In 1948, Louis Saint-Laurent—remembered by all Canadians as "Papa Pavement"—ran for public office on a promise of connecting east and west by a single continuous thoroughfare. Although he couldn't campaign more than a few kilometres from his hometown, he won in a landslide. Immediately after the disastrous victory parade, he set about making the dream a reality. Unfortunately, during highway construction, he was killed by a landslide.

Sparsely populated Prince Edward Island was chosen as the site for the experimental first stretch of the project. The "Road to Avonlea" still attracts a steady stream of Japanese and German tourists, all eager to marvel at our disciplined engineering. Unfortunately, toxins that leached out of the early road surface caused terrible harm to the local population, and Islanders continue to suffer from the pale skin and red hair caused by "Highway Fever."

Over the next decade, one province after another was connected to the Trans-Canada Highway. Fortunate towns through which the route passed experienced rapid growth and the arrival of NHL hockey. Those bypassed by the route became cultural backwaters, doomed to be forgotten unless a cherubic pop sensation were to miraculously emerge, half a century later, from amongst the filth.

The "TCH" plays such an important role in Canadian cultural life that it has given rise to many words and expressions that pepper Canada's distinctive dialects. It's not uncommon to hear a Canadian refer to a "Manitoba Straightaway" or an "Elliot Lake Turnoff" in everyday conversation. In Quebec, where the highway is known as "l'autoroute Québécois," every youngster can recite a nursery rhyme about a mischievous driver named Jacques who deliberately makes it difficult for anybody with out-of-province licence plates to merge.

Visitors to Canada who drive any length of the fabled highway quickly discover that nearly every 1/100th of a megametre brings a new surprise. The countless roadside attractions and curiosities found along the Trans-Canada Highway are sure to delight even the most jaded traveller.

Wawa, Ontario: Visitors flock to this remote northern town, home to the world's largest fibreglass goose sculpture, to pay homage to Canada's most famous fowl.

Lloydminster, Alberta and Saskatchewan: This prairie twin city, straddling the Alberta/Saskatchewan border, offers exactly double the fun. A rare twin-lane section of the highway takes you into town, where two-for-one deals are the norm and every bed is a double bed. While you're there, enjoy a double-double—or two! Lloydminster is also home to Canada's largest conjoined-twins museum.

Moncton, New Brunswick: Just off the highway you can visit the famed "Magnetic Hill," where a strange optical illusion makes it appear as if you are actually in Edmundston, New Brunswick.

The Trans-Canada Highway is more than just a road—it's a symbol of Canada and its people. Through both Canadian seasons, the highway connects the entire nation. From east to west, all Canadians can call the road their own. It belongs as much to Newfoundlanders as it does to relocated Alberta Newfoundlanders. This vital vein sustains an entire people; without it, there could be no Swollen Members concert tour, and the Beer Store would be impossibly out of reach. Put simply, the Trans-Canada Highway is Canada (just ask Tom Cochrane).

Who's Driving on the
Trans-Canada Highway?

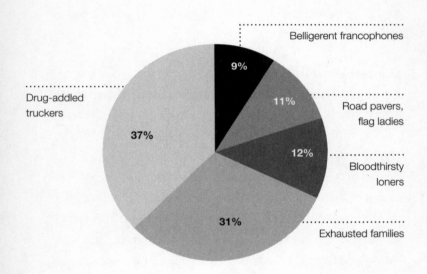

Belligerent francophones

Drug-addled
truckers

Road pavers,
flag ladies

37%

9%

11%

12%

Bloodthirsty
loners

31%

Exhausted families

Canada's Surface Area

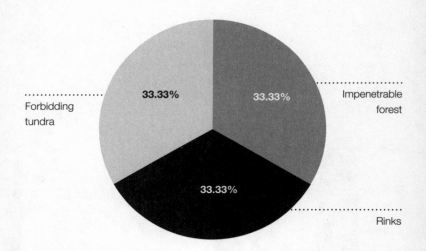

Tallest Structures by Province

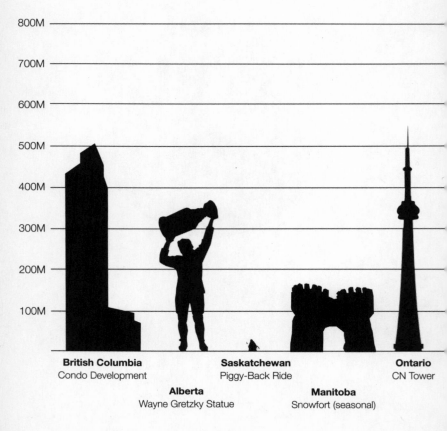

800M	
700M	
600M	
500M	
400M	
300M	
200M	
100M	

British Columbia
Condo Development

Alberta
Wayne Gretzky Statue

Saskatchewan
Piggy-Back Ride

Manitoba
Snowfort (seasonal)

Ontario
CN Tower

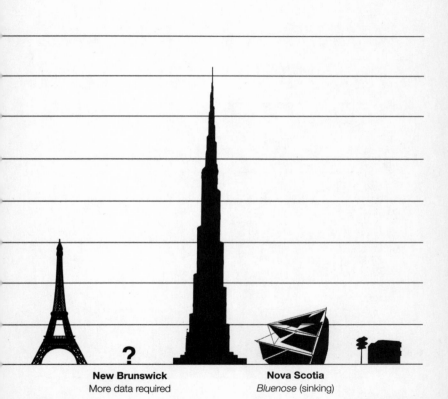

New Brunswick
More data required

Nova Scotia
Bluenose (sinking)

Quebec
Eiffel Tower

P.E.I.
Avonlea Tower

**Newfoundland
and Labrador**
2-Storey Tim Hortons

Total Number of Canadas

Gentrification in Canada

Canada's cities and towns have gone through a multitude of changes over the last 20 years. As the Canadian economy has shifted from producing goods to offering services, wealth has migrated into the cities. With this wealth comes increased coffee prices, taller buildings, and adult bicyclists.

As neighbourhoods gentrify they become more uniform, losing elements that make them unique and making way for efficient housing and chain restaurants. This leaves the original residents of the area struggling to stand out from the rest, leading to neighbourhood rivalries. This inevitably results in things like competitive dog walking, fashionable yet insulting graffiti, and wine fights.

Gentrification affects cities across Canada in different ways. What follows are some gentrification case studies from around the country.

Case Study: The Ossington Strip—Toronto, ON

The Ossington Strip, located in West Toronto, has gone through extreme changes over the last 10 years. What started as a Portuguese and Vietnamese neighbourhood soon became an entertainment district, and again transformed into a catch-all for aging club rats. It went from storage rental units, to quirky restaurants, to full-blown dance clubs in less than a decade.

This effect is known as the "Jimmy Principle." Take Jimmy, a moderately attractive male in his mid-20s making $60–75K per year. Jimmy has grown tired of the club scene downtown and is looking for more interesting (that is, lower-income) people to spend his Saturday nights with. He ventures to the Ossington Strip because he likes girls who wear glasses. Jimmy does not want to go alone, so he brings his friend Doug. Doug's girlfriend Becky doesn't like it when Jimmy and Doug get together, so she tags along for good measure. Becky brings some of her young, attractive female friends, all of whom typically patronize the downtown club scene, so she doesn't feel like a third wheel. The mixture of people in the bars is now 50% interesting people and 50% Jimmys, Dougs, and Beckys. This is gentrification in action.

Case Study: East Hastings—Vancouver, BC

East Hastings, the centre of meth activity in Canada, is famous for its aversion to gentrification. Upscale businesses that attempt to move into East Hastings are quickly vandalized by local vagrants, in an effort to keep rent prices low. Being such an expensive city to live in, Vancouver residents are motivated to maintain the status quo.

With the exception of Vancouver, Victoria, and Kelowna, the province of British Columbia has a right-leaning population, suspicious of change. BC is driven by industries such as logging, skinning, and mountain maintenance, which are primarily family-run businesses impervious to fluctuations in the economy. The trends in these small BC communities are mirroring those of East Hastings, although driven by completely different politics. Stats Canada will continue to investigate these trends, in the interest of documenting the similarities between loggers and meth enthusiasts.

Case Study: Sissy's Motors—Charlottetown, PEI

Charlottetown has recently been flooded with big-box stores, at the request of the citizens; a referendum was held after a majority of the population expressed dissatisfaction with local "mom-and-pop" establishments. One establishment in particular was Sissy's Motors, a car dealership whose owner refused to sell vehicles that were not 100% manufactured in Canada. In past decades this didn't pose a problem, but the recent decline in Canadian manufacturing capacity has greatly narrowed the wares Sissy has been able to sell. The business now stocks only Quebec-made bicycles, and Sissy becomes enraged when people ask about buying a car. Scenarios like this are why the public has requested that big-box stores move in to replace local vendors. (It doesn't help that Sissy is openly disdainful of Islanders afflicted with "Highway Fever.")

Did You Know?

3 out of 5 great lakes are really just okay lakes.

Top Five Vacation Spots in New Brunswick

1.
2.
3.
4.
5.

*More data required

Top Ghost Towns

According to a survey conducted by Stats Canada in 1994, the 20 most least-inhabited towns in Canada are as follows:

- Alberta II, Northwest Territories
- Iron Shanty, Alberta
- Leaky Dam, Ontario
- Whispering Evil, Manitoba
- Dead Bull, New Brunswick
- Rough Patch, BC
- Wasp Attack, Alberta
- Dripping Sword, Manitoba
- Snake Trap, Nova Scotia
- Haunted Train, Ontario
- Scorching Ant, Newfoundland and Labrador

- Scorching Aunt, Newfoundland and Labrador

- Poop Poop 123, Nunavut

- Unrelentless, Ontario

- Diefenbakersville, Saskatchewan

- Dead Boat Captain, PEI

- Drake, Ontario

- Undiscovered, Yukon

- Deer Face, Alberta

- Crotch Gulch, Saskatchewan

 Did You Know?

91% of people living in the Canadian prairies were tricked into living there.

Where Is Brunch?

Top Newsworthy Events in Labrador

Date	Headline
June 7, 1978	Cat rescued from tree; Suzy MacDonald elated
June 6, 1980	New flag
May 19, 1993	"What is Labrador?" answer on last night's Final Jeopardy
December 19, 1997	Slice of French toast resembles Jean Chrétien
December 31, 1999	Labrador immune to Y2K scare: no computers
August 23, 2010	Temperature reaches historic high of –23ºC; global warming suspected

Wolves vs. Ironic Wolf Shirts, 1867–2017

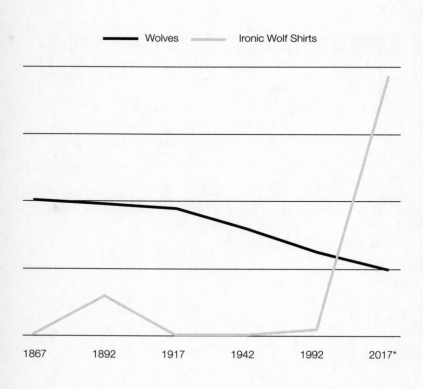

1867	1892	1917	1942	1992	2017*

Wolves ——— Ironic Wolf Shirts

*estimate

Common Misspellings of Canadian City Names

Red Deer, Alberta
Red Dear
Read Deer
Read Dear

Toronto, Ontario
T-rana
Tornado
Tomato

Saint John, New Brunswick
St. John's
Taint Ron's
Saint Jon

Sydney, Nova Scotia
Sidknee
Sidney Crosby
Cidd

Iqaluit, Nunavut
Icaluit
Iqaluweed
Iqaluwheat
Icicle
Dsadkjjjowuqw
Jdsakdjasdjajjaaanuit
Icalutweet
Calaweed
Whitehorse
Aaaaaaaaahhhhhju
Your Pal, Louie
Iiiiiigloo
Turkmenistan
Salmon Arm
A Calculator
Kijiji

Agriculture of New Brunswick

*More data required

Canada's Top Five Islands

Baffin Island

Canada's largest island was engineered in 1887 to get the polar bears out of Churchill, Manitoba, and is made completely out of discarded Bay Christmas catalogues. The largest city, Iqaluit, is the capital of Nunavut, with a population of 6,145, most of whom are snowmen. The most exciting thing to ever happen on the island was the day it was named Canada's largest island.

Vancouver Island

Vancouver Island didn't become part of Canada until 1995's barely publicized "Patchouli War," which started and ended with a handshake. This island is where most elderly Canadians go to die. It also is home to Mile 0 of the Trans-Canada Highway—or Mile 4,990 (7,821 km), if your glass is half empty.

Ellesmere Island

Canada's northernmost island is populated by 146 people, all of them once children who ran away to live with Santa Claus and couldn't find their way back home. The record-high temperature in this area happened in May 1999 when the thermometer hit a scorching +22°C, at which time, tragically, everyone became homeless when their houses melted.

Prince Edward Island

This island is best known for the beloved character from Canadian literature Anne of Green Gables. Because 87% of the population are redheads, the island is projected to become a ghost town by 2060. (The other 13% of the population are potatoes.) PEI is also the only province whose letters can be rearranged to form the name of a delicious treat.

The Thousand Islands

This grouping of 1,864 islands is best known for their popular salad dressing, which is the only option at any Ontario restaurant. People who attempt to use their own dressing will be escorted from the building and have their bottle confiscated and immediately destroyed. The Thousand Islands is the second most popular item Canada shares with the United States after Ryan Gosling.

Noteworthy, but not good enough:

Newfoundland

This island is nicknamed "The Rock," probably after the WWE wrestler. For more on Newfoundland, see page 138.

Did You Know?

37% of Prince Edward Island still uses dial-up Internet by choice.

Discover: Vancouver

Surrounded by many natural wonders—mountains, oceans, trees, bears—the people of Vancouver are known as the most outdoorsy in Canada (which may also be why the rest of Canada thinks the city has a "homeless problem"). In fact, 72% of Vancouverites live outdoors to be closer to nature.

Because of their love of the outdoors, clothing (or "gear," in local parlance) meant for outside activities is 89% more likely to sell in Vancouver than in any other Canadian city: fleece pullovers, rugged trousers, and Teva™ sandals are collectively known as the "Official Uniform of Vancouver."

There is a negative side to spending the majority of the time outside in Vancouver. Since Vancouver receives only an average of seven minutes of sunshine per day, its residents run a high risk of getting caught in the rain.[1] However, this is only perceived as a risk by the rest of the country, because the people of Vancouver

---

1 In a related statistic, 91% of Vancouver residents say they like piña coladas.

in fact really enjoy the rain. Vancouver spends 8% of its GDP on rain protection tools. The city is home to more than one hundred million umbrellas and is 77% more likely to sell ponchos than any other major city across Canada. A little rain is not likely to keep Vancouverites away from their precious outdoors.

History

The city of Vancouver was incorporated on April 6, 1886.
That same year the entire city was razed by the now infamous Vancouver Fire. The residents of Vancouver were forced to flee into the mountains, above the city's flames, which became the first recorded hike on Canadian soil. Hiking is now the second most popular activity in Vancouver (behind being self-important).

Geography

Vancouver has one of the largest urban parks in North America, Stanley Park. The park covers 404.9 hectares and is home to 15,000 squirrels, 1,750 bears, countless crows, and 1,342 lost tourists.[2] The city also sits on one of the world's major bodies of water, the Pacific Ocean. This ocean is known for having some whales in it.

---

2 The majority of these lost tourists are eventually found, having survived on half-empty Starbucks coffees, discarded nature bars, and the occasional fire-roasted squirrel.

Discover: Salmon Arm

Established in 1905, Salmon Arm is one of Canada's fastest-growing cities. Salmon Arm, or "City of Bridges," as it is more commonly called, is the jewel of British Columbia. The name Salmon Arm comes from the mythical salmon creature named Salmon Pete, a half salmon/half human with the arms of a man and the smell of a fish. Contrary to popular belief, Salmon Arm is home to zero salmon. However, black bears outnumber humans four to one (although this ratio is not uncommon for cities in British Columbia).

Economy

Bursting at the seams with more than three hotels and two beaches, Salmon Arm is world famous and known for being Canada's fourth most popular vacation destination despite the frequent bear attacks. With a growing population of more than 17,000 black bears, Salmon Arm is Canada's most densely populated bear-ea (bear area). Many residents of Salmon Arm live in constant fear of bear attacks and avoid leaving the house. In a direct correlation, mommy blogging has become one of the preferred career choices for many Salmonites. Some other preferred careers are bear whispering and bear hugging.

Sports and Recreation

In their spare time, Salmonites flock to the countless fenced-in public parks and the two mid-sized sports arenas, where the bear situation is heavily monitored.

Salmon Arm is home to one minor hockey team, the Salmon Arm Maulers, and a burgeoning indoor soccer league with its undefeated team, the Salmon Arm Salmons. In addition to these teams, Salmon Arm has also founded the first-ever bear–human crossover sport, known as "Play Dead!"

Discover: Edmonton

According to the 2011 census Edmonton has a population of approximately 812,000 people, making it the fifth-largest municipality in Canada. Approximately 67% of that number can be attributed to the constant flux of shoppers passing through the famous West Edmonton Mall. The WEM was the world's largest mall when it opened, and while it held that title until 2004 it has since fallen to 10th place. Its attractions include the world's second-largest indoor water park, an ice palace, a shooting range, an hourly public re-enactment of Wayne Gretzky's wedding, and a few shops here and there.

History

Edmonton was established by Europeans in 1795, when a couple of prospectors got lost on their way to what is now known as British Columbia. However, the first people to inhabit the land were there around 3,000 BC and perhaps as early as 12,000 BC. Back then the area was prime for mastodon (a.k.a. woolly mammoth) hunting.

Climate

Every year approximately 35 people die in Edmonton from exposure to extreme cold (21% of the cases happen between June and August). The average resident of Edmonton wears three pairs of socks, two sets of mittens, four scarves, and nine tuques just to combat the chill.

The coldest temperature ever recorded in Edmonton was –98°C, in 1999. An all-Canadian boy band was formed and named after this day: –98 Degrees spent four years in the MuchMusic Top Ten with their song "Baby, I Wanna Stay Warm with You Under My Thermal Duvet."

 Did You Know?

Every 14 seconds a Canadian pretends they didn't see another Canadian slip on sidewalk ice.

What's in a Calgarian's Closet?

Calgary is known for a lot of things. Oil, a half-assed tower, and urban cowboys. Calgarians, as a people, hold on to things truly and deeply, like the '88 Olympics and that time the Flames were good at scoring. To get a deeper look into Calgarian culture, we chose 100 homes at random and excavated their closets to examine what makes a true Calgarian.

- 17 belts with buckles
- A collection of Ralph Klein bobbleheads
- Day of the week cowboy hats
- Giant giraffe won at the Stampede in 1997
- A box of Flutie Flakes
- $300 hockey stick (never used)
- Dinosaur fossils
- Autographed Joel Otto jersey

- Trophy from neighbourhood calf-roping competition
- '88 Olympic mascot head (Hidy)
- The cowboy boot not lost in the parking lot of "COWBOYS" nightclub
- Stephen Harper election sign
- Stephen Harper protest sign
- I Heart Alberta Beef poster
- *Cool Runnings* VHS tape

Did You Know?

Western Canada consumes five times more Nickelback than Eastern Canada.

Least Popular Slogans
for Saskatchewan

According to a tourism survey conducted in 1987, the top 10 least-effective provincial slogans were the following:

- Saskatchewan: For lovers who love wheat
- Saskatchewan: Flat like a delicious crêpe
- Saskatchewan: Now serving crêpes
- Saskatchewan: You guys love wheat?
- Saskatchewan: Are we having fun yet?
- Saskatchewan: We don't need hockey to have fun!
- Saskatchewan: We named Saskatoon after a fruit
- Saskatchewan: Home to four horses and one tractor
- Saskatchewan: Tell them Doug sent you!
- Saskatchewan: More fun than New Brunswick—we promise

Discover: Saskatoon

Saskatoon has many sights and attractions to offer its residents and tourists, such as the Mendel Art Gallery, Prairieland Park, and Midtown Plaza. Unfortunately, these attractions are available at most only two months of the year; for the other ten months everything is covered in a layer of ice and snow.

Saskatoon is Saskatchewan's largest metropolitan city, at around 260,000 residents. Even though Saskatoon is technically considered metropolitan, 87% of its residents are wheat farmers.

Because most of its population is made up of farmers, Saskatoon's local diners, cafés, and bars are very forgiving with their no-animals policies. Saskatoon is the only city in Canada where you are allowed to have a nice sit-down meal with your favourite livestock. In fact, Saskatoon's premier '50s-style diner, Broadway Café, gets 16% of all its revenue from various farm animals.

Geography

The highest point in Saskatoon, at 0.25 metres, is the speed bump in the Briarwood neighbourhood. Saskatoon is so flat there is never any worry of cars rolling away when parked; as such, only one in every ten thousand cars has an emergency brake installed. This saves on automobile costs, making the average car $4,500 less expensive than vehicles in the rest of Canada. These savings are offset by the similar amount most Saskatonians will spend every winter to get their cars jump-started after forgetting to plug them in overnight.

Economy

Saskatoon is the leading city in Canada in terms of farming supplies. However, it falls far behind in other industries such as retail and fast food. Saskatoon was without a Starbucks until 2005. Coincidentally, the average daily amount spent on coffee that year went from $1.75 to $7.80. As well, Saskatoon has zero Taco Bells. (Compare this to a city of similar size, Oshawa, Ontario, which has five to seven Taco Bells.) Tragically, with no Taco Bells, only 3–4% of Saskatonians have ever tasted a Fries Supreme.

Provincial Profile: Manitoba

Stretching from the edge of the Arctic to the fringe of the prairies, Manitoba is at the heart of our great nation. And for this reason, doctors insist that Manitoba should take better care of itself because all that snow shovelling is going to give Canada a heart attack. Take it easy, you guys.

Too far west to be an eastern province, and too poor to be a western province, Manitoba is a land of polar opposites: the temperature swings nearly 100°C between winter and summer, and the land itself is divided between fertile farmland and desolate tundra. Manitoba's licence plate promises that its people are friendly, but visitors to Winnipeg are statistically almost guaranteed to have their car broken into.

Like the rest of Canada, Manitoba is a land of immigrants. Many Manitobans trace their roots to a good-natured 19th-century prank that tricked tens of thousands of Eastern European homesteaders into moving to this backbreaking hinterland.

Recent census data, however, reveal that 11% of Manitobans are actually just dense swarms of mosquitoes.

Manitoba's early years were prosperous, but the decline of the railroad and the Great Depression hit the province hard. This is evidenced by the fact that on most money circulating in Manitoba the Queen looks about 29 years old.

Every spring, Manitoba transforms from a prairie province into an outpost of the Maritimes as the flooding Red River turns much of the province into a soggy insect nursery. If you are reading this book in Manitoba right now, there's a 45% chance it's damp.

Winnipeg, home to 60% of the province's population, has the unique distinction of being the planet's Slurpee capital. Despite bone-shattering Arctic air in the winter and straw-clogging clouds of bugs in the summer, Winnipeggers consume more coloured sugarwater than anybody in the world. Winnipeg's affection for the icy drink was immortalized in the 1975 Burton Cummings soft-rock classic "Slurpee Juice (Gotta Gotta Have It)."

Never one to back down from a fight, these pugnacious prairie folk sparked the Red River Rebellion, the Winnipeg General Strike, and the long and deadly struggle to bring the Jets back to town.

It's hard to imagine Canada without Manitoba, although it would definitely shave a few hours off most road trips. The geographic centre of Canada, Manitoba is also located at the statistical middle: the average Canadian is "Chad from Brandon."

Did You Know?

56% of Manitobans are convinced they've travelled to the future when visiting other provinces.

Population of Canada,
Measured in Units of Ontarios

One Ontario

One Ontario

One Ontario

Where Do Canadians Live?

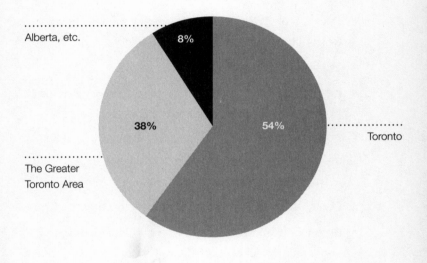

Alberta, etc.

8%

38%

54%

Toronto

The Greater
Toronto Area

Reasons the Rest of Canada Hates Ontario

- Ontario stole Yukon's boyfriend even though Yukon told Ontario that, like, they were totally getting serious

- Ontario is SUCH a drama queen

- Ever since Ontario became the most populous province in the country, it's been acting really stuck-up

- At British Columbia's winter dance Ontario got so drunk and puked on Alberta's plaid vest and never even apologized or offered to dry clean it

- Ontario said Quebec looked fat in hoop earrings

- Even though they've met like 7 times, Ontario always pretends it doesn't know Nunavut

- Ontario only ever writes "k" in text messages

- Yukon thinks Ontario is kind of passive-aggressive and it didn't want to say anything so it left a note asking Ontario to please stop being so stuck-up thanks

- Ontario said Ryan Gosling would never go for Nova Scotia

- None of the other provinces understand why Ontario gets so much attention. It's not even that pretty or interesting or cool.

Did You Know?

Toronto experiences an average of 28 smug alert days annually.

Ontario's Most Famous Destinations

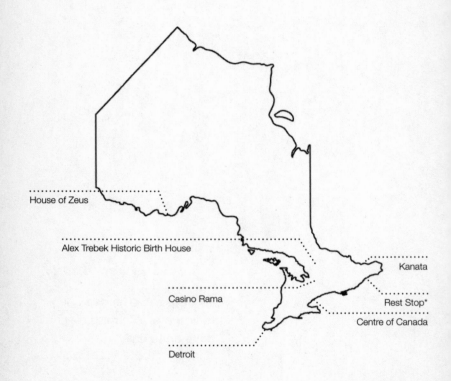

House of Zeus

Alex Trebek Historic Birth House

Casino Rama

Detroit

Kanata

Rest Stop*

Centre of Canada

*Capital of Jamaica

Things Torontonians Care About

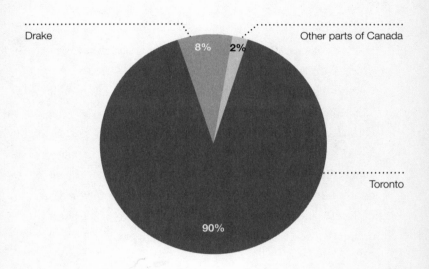

Drake

Other parts of Canada

8% 2%

Toronto

90%

Discover: Ottawa

Ottawa, Ontario (not to be confused with Ottawa, Illinois), is the political capital of Canada. The city has been home to Canada's greatest political leaders, most notably Prime Minister Kim Campbell, Prime Minister John Diefenbaker, and Speaker of the House [name unknown]. As well as being the nation's capital, Ottawa is also the capital of beaver tails, a delicious fried pastry. The dessert makes up 78% of the average Ottawan's nutritional intake. Eating that much deep-fried food in any other city would cause a 64% increase in obesity and diabetes, but the residents of Ottawa are able to maintain a healthy lifestyle by ice skating on the Rideau Canal approximately 4 hours per day.

Geography

Ottawa sits on the Ottawa River and is regionally considered to be Eastern Ontario; however, 82% of Ontarians consider it to be The North.

The Ottawa River divides Ontario and Quebec, which is why the Ottawa River is the most revered river in all of Canada.

Located on a major but mostly dormant fault line, Ottawa has been known to be mildly annoyed by earthquakes from time to time. In the great earthquake of 2010, 17 lawn chairs were knocked over, 3 ambassadors spilled their coffees, 24 framed pictures of the Queen fell from the wall, and countless dogs were later found hiding under tables.

Sports

Ottawa is very busy with politics and sitting in the House of Commons, which does not leave a lot of time for sports. Unlike other major metropolitan cities, like Toronto (which has four professional sports teams), Ottawa has only one and a half professional sports teams (the Ottawa Senators and the Ottawa REDBLACKS). However, few city residents ever attend home games because they are too busy embezzling public funds and setting up slush accounts.

Provincial Profile: Quebec

Quebec was officially founded as a province of Canada in 1774. Prior to this, the area known as Quebec was largely uninhabited by humans. However, there were a large number of ducks living on this land, which are the real reason why Quebec came to be.

Around the same time, the English had been settling around Upper Canada, on the other side of the St. Lawrence River. As they were close to the border of what is now Quebec, the English were able to hear the quacking of the great number of ducks living off the land. Knowing very little of the French culture, and caring even less, the English mistook the ducks' noise for a conversation spoken in French. They were convinced the French had arrived in Canada and were attempting to settle. This caused much unrest amongst the English. On April 25, 1773, Sir Thomas Gerrard sent word to England of the French settlement.

Not willing to go to war, the English government sent a letter of negotiation to the French King asking him to call his men back to France. The French King, however, was completely unaware of this Canadian colony (mostly because the colony was a waddling of ducks), but did not want to admit this. He thought he would look unorganized and unaware of his country's colonization missions. So, to hide his ignorance, the King replied to the English, "I will not back down: We, the great country of France, were there first. In fact, not only am I not asking my men to return, I am sending even more men to aid in this settlement! *Au revoir, Sir!*"

So the King of France sent a colony of a few thousand people to settle Quebec; they arrived on January 12, 1774. To the settlers' surprise Quebec was considerably colder than France. They sent a request to the King to return home, as they "hated it here." Not willing to look like a fool, the King denied the men their return. He wanted to ensure that Quebec was populated, otherwise the English may find out he didn't know what he was doing. So, these few thousand men and women became the first colony of Quebec. Upon hearing that they would not be able to return to their home country the settlers decreed Quebec's official motto to be *"Je me souviens,"* meaning "I remember (when we were banished to this hellishly cold province and not allowed to return to France)"—and thereby creating the France/Quebec relationship of Quebec wanting to be France and France wanting nothing to do with Quebec.

Discover: Montreal

Montreal was originally called Ville-Marie (The City of Mary), but the Quebecois quickly grew tired of having to translate it for the rest of the country. The name was changed to reflect the triple-peaked hill located in the heart of the city (Mount Royal).

Montreal is known as "Canada's Cultural Capital," but only by one-quarter of the country (the one-quarter who live in Quebec). For the most part, Montreal is known to 93% of 18-year-old Ontarians as "The City I Can Legally Drink In."

Economy

Montreal's economy is largely dependent on cheese (*fromage, en français*) and cheese product exports. Montreal is the number-one distributor of cheese curds used for poutine. On the Montreal Exchange (MX) cheese makes up 87% of all financial trades, with the majority being in cheese futures.

Montreal also has a large market for stripping and other adult entertainment. Twenty-four-hour gentlemen's clubs make up

18% of Quebec's gross domestic product (GDP), making it Canada's sexiest GDP.

Culture

Montreal is heavily influenced by the French culture. It is the second-largest primarily French-speaking city in the world next to Paris, making it the largest city not to be understood by the rest of Canada. Tourists are six times more likely to need a French–English dictionary while travelling to Montreal than anywhere else in the world.

Montreal is Canada's centre for French-language radio and television broadcasting. The top five television shows broadcast from Montreal are *Just For Laughs: Gags, Deux ans et demi hommes, Bleu nuit, MétéoMédia*, and *Nuit de l'hockey dans Canada*.

Discover: Halifax

The City of Halifax is the capital of Nova Scotia. It is also the largest city in Atlantic Canada, with a population of 1,200 residents (4% of which are various sea creatures). It became internationally famous when the citizens of Halifax elected a cat as mayor—making it the third capital city in Canada to have a feline politician.

History

The city's defining historical event was the Halifax Explosion. The explosion occurred when a ship importing Diet Coke collided with another ship with a full cargo of Mentos (The Fresh Maker). The fizzy disaster claimed the lives of approximately 2,000 residents and countless lobsters. To this day it is illegal to mix Mentos and Diet Coke in Halifax and the crime is punishable by public humiliation.

Geography

Halifax is 5,490 km^2, 84% of which is the Atlantic Ocean. It is the only city in Canada to be primarily underwater. This is especially beneficial to the large crab and lobster population, as they prefer to live in the sea.

At the centre of the city is a very large hill, named Citadel Hill, upon which the city was founded. Although the hill was originally used for military purposes it is now primarily used to consume alcohol on. Most of Halifax's major pubs and bars are on the street leading up to the peak. Haligonians have made it a tradition to start their drinking at the bottom of the hill and finish at the top. This is why 93% of the city's drunks can always be found on top of Citadel Hill.

Did You Know?

The average Canadian financial transaction produces 9 kg of change.

Provincial Profile:
Newfoundland and Labrador

Canada's westernleast province, Newfoundland and Labrador is a land of statistical peculiarities. It's the youngest province in Confederation but, thanks to the generation that left to find their fortune in the western oil patch, its people are the oldest. It was the first place Europeans visited in North America, yet it is the last place most North Americans would want to end up. It is the most linguistically diverse place in Canada, but its people are the least comprehensible.

This starkly beautiful land, where the unemployment percentage is high and the alcohol percentage is higher, is the only province whose official flower is a rock.

While the Viking encampment at L'Anse aux Meadows died out quickly (its brave settlers are thought to have suffered from malnutrition after arriving with nothing but the ingredients for campfire s'mores), Europeans returned to Newfoundland's jagged shores at the end of the 15th century. John Cabot quickly discovered that the sea's bountiful (fish) harvest more than made up for the comically infertile soil on the cliffs above. In the years that followed Cabot's visit, homely Newfoundland was the belle of the North Atlantic ball as Portuguese, French, Basque, and English expeditions all competed for access to the riches beneath her waterline. Any resistance to settlement melted away after a triangular trade route between Newfoundland, Europe, and the West Indies introduced the island to cheap and potent Jamaican rum.

As a colony of England, Newfoundland enjoyed the standard perks of British rule: arm's-length governance and an obligation to die in a faraway battle. By the 1930s Newfoundland was struggling to overcome massive debts and persistent fish-breath. A period of political turmoil preceded the 1949 vote to join Canada, a sort of bizarro-land version of the Quebec referendum where the funny-talking people want in.

The local economy was decimated in the 1990s by the collapse of the cod fishery and the discontinuation of the McDonald's McCod sandwich. These difficult times were marked by population decline, high unemployment, and exactly the same rate of liquor consumption as always. That dark fog has lifted, however, as the economy has rebounded significantly in recent years. Energy production and iTunes sales of Great Big Sea songs have injected record amounts of beer money into the local economy.

While Newfoundlanders will tell you that they live by the rhythms of the sea, daily life in the province is influenced even more by its odd time zone. Television shows start a half-hour later than everywhere else in the country, and young drivers are instructed to keep their hands at 10:30 and 2:30. This peculiar quirk of the clock has been immortalized in the classic Gordon Lightfoot song "Thirty Minute Man."

Across the Straits of Quebec, Newfoundland's borders extend to a sparsely inhabited mainland backwater called Labrador. Few expected that those very backwaters would pay off centuries later once the hydro dam was invented. A 2001 amendment to the Constitution of Canada changed the province's official name to Newfoundland and Labrador, a union that held particular significance, as many Newfoundlanders consider lowly Labrador to be "the Newfoundland of Newfoundland."

Long ignored by the rest of Canada, Newfoundland has recently become a booming destination for domestic tourists. Visitors from the rest of the country are flocking to "The Rock" to experience the striking landscape and stomach-churning cuisine for themselves. It's estimated that the average first-time visitor to St. John's will kiss 0.9 cods, will spend 35 minutes on or around Signal Hill, and will walk the entire length of George Street 2.3 times looking for the way back to the hotel.

Our statistics suggest that Newfoundland's winning streak will extend well into the 21st century. While the effects of climate change turn the rest of the country into a barren, lifeless land exposed to nature's harshest whims, Newfoundlanders won't flinch. While droughts threaten to force Canadians to give up fresh produce and nutritious vegetables, Newfoundlanders will gnaw happily on bog apples like nothing is wrong. As water levels rise, forcing humanity to move to apocalyptic floating refuges, Newfoundlanders will appreciate the free upgrade. Like a lighthouse in the fog, Newfoundland will guide Canada through a very uncertain future.

Newfoundland Map

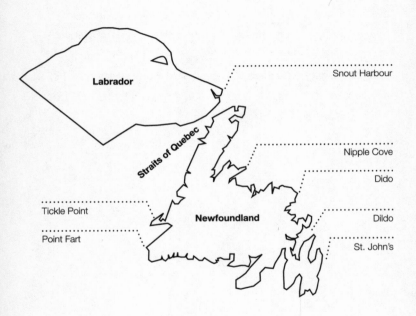

Labrador

Snout Harbour

Straits of Quebec

Nipple Cove

Dido

Tickle Point

Newfoundland

Dildo

Point Fart

St. John's

Weather

AND THE

Environment

A Statistically Average
Canadian Weather Forecast

Canadian Weather: A History

Canadians understand the common perception that their homeland is constantly covered in a blurry tundra of death and emptiness. For 90% of its residents, this is 100% true. At times, Canada basically becomes the scary part of Narnia (which our research indicates is how Sarnia, Ontario, got its name).

Canadians face insurmountable feats of nature year-round, and have developed many tools to protect themselves accordingly. These tools primarily take advantage of nature, such as jackets made of geese, stylish body hair, and of course, multi-level igloos. Even these are rarely required since Canadians are typically quite proud of being cold. Historically, the first people of Canada had many uses for the animals and nature around them, but very few of those uses were clothes. They were not ashamed of uncovered bodies, nor were they ashamed of their local hockey[1] team. Canadians soon grew a thick skin when it

---

1 This was field hockey, or as it was known in the early days of Canada, "Hit Squirrel with Spear."

came to the elements. It was only when the Europeans arrived that Canadians learned the restrictive nature of pelt and silk.

It was the arrival of the Europeans that introduced not only smallpox and measles to Canada, but also frostbite and hypothermia. Up to that point, Canadians could walk in the snow for days on end, tracking buffalo and women they weren't related to. This incredible resistance to the natural world was slowly bred out of Canadians through the generations, which explains Toronto traffic in January.

So what effect does this storied heritage have on modern Canadians? The primary influence is on our language. "Tuque" isn't a word outside of Canada. The word "ice" now appears in every brand of Canadian beer. We still have 50 words for "snow," but they are now European curse words.

Each province has a unique terrain, and therefore a unique weather pattern. For example:

Saskatchewan: open plains offer no shelter from the cold.

British Columbia: mountainous terrain focuses and amplifies the cold.

Ontario: the Great Lakes are a great source of cold.

Quebec: chilly personalities offer no respite from the cold.

Alberta: the cold has migrated here from Atlantic Canada.

New Brunswick: [More research required.]

Studies have shown that Canadians take pride in cold weather. 80% of Canadian sports involve ice. 65% of Canadians prefer a "bunny hug" to a human hug. 71% of Canadian fathers will barbecue until late January. 0% of Canadians will admit that it's cold out.

Did You Know?

4 out of 5 Canadians spend 7 hours a day commenting on the weather.

Percentage of Manitoba
Currently Covered by Snow

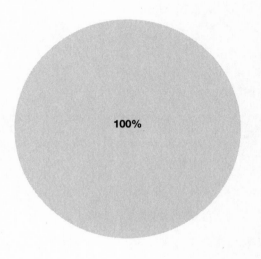

100%

Ways That Canada
Is Similar to Outer Space

Ways That Canada Is Similar to Outer Space

- Cold

- Mostly empty

- Can see for an infinite distance (prairie provinces only)

- Americans learn about it in high school and immediately forget everything

- Russians have visited

- Takes a long time to get anywhere

- Long periods of uninterrupted darkness

- Often looks like a computer desktop picture

- Exposed skin freezes immediately

- Nobody can hear you scream

Ways That Canada Isn't Similar to Outer Space

- Movies that take place in space are usually successful
- America and Russia didn't fight over Canada
- The Inuit

 Did You Know?

63% of Yellowknife residents might as well be living in space.

How Long Is
a Canadian Month?

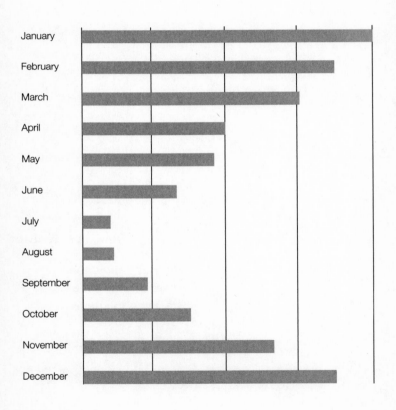

January				
February				
March				
April				
May				
June				
July				
August				
September				
October				
November				
December				

Weather: A Canadian Conversation of Choice

Small talk is an important part of office life in Canada; it's a way to bond with people you wouldn't want to see outside of work, and a way of establishing solid workplace relationships. Not all topics are safe to bring up, though—those to be avoided include politics, religion, and finances. These subjects will require lengthy, personal, and intimate conversations. The Canadian ideal is to seem friendly while not really caring at all. It is for this reason that 73% of all conversations in the workplace are about weather. Talking about weather requires no value judgments, only mere empirical observations. Stats Canada has compiled the top three weather conversations and has outlined them as follows to help you, the average Canadian, fare well around the office water cooler.

At work, 32% of all weather conversations revolve around precipitation or possible precipitation. If it is raining/snowing outside it is a good idea to comment on said rain/snow. If no precipitation is occurring you are free to comment on the upcoming possibility. "It looks clear out now, but I hear it is supposed to precipitate later today, Jim." Talking about precipitation is a great because no matter what the weather is like you have something to say about it.

The next most popular topic is temperature, at 29% of all weather conversations in a Canadian office setting. Temperature is as versatile as precipitation because no matter what it is you can comment on it. If it's mild you can rhetorically say, "Isn't the temperature just perfect, Suzy?" If it's hot say something like, "What a scorcher out there, eh Gord?" And, of course, if it's cold you can merely exclaim "Brrrrr" followed by a lighthearted chuckle.

The third most popular weather topic for the Canadian workplace is windchill. Although it applies only during the winter season it still inspires 23% of all weather conversations. Canadians as a people do not like windchill, so negatively commenting on it will cost you no friends in the office. Something like, "Sure, it's only −11 outside, but with the windchill it feels like −73. I'm definitely not going out there today, Mary." This will give you on average one to two minutes of conversation without ever having to go into anything personal.

If you stick to these topics of conversation, Stats Canada predicts your quality of life in the office will increase by 7 to 9%.

A Guide to Cold Poles
and Your Tongue

Canada is below zero degrees (Celsius) upward of 75% of the time. As such, metal objects—particularly posts (goal, lamp, etc.)—are frozen for the better part of the year. A common prank is to persuade a friend to lick one of these frozen poles, leading to his tongue being stuck to said pole. In 2011 alone, 237,500 Canadians' tongues were stuck to a pole at some time during the winter season. In addition, 78% of these "incidents" happened to Canadian children ages 5 through 11 while on recess at school.

Given the staggering number of Canadians who are tricked into this, Stats Canada has put together a best practices guide to unsticking your tongue from a pole in winter. If you find yourself with your tongue on a cold, metal pole in the winter simply follow these steps to free your mouth:

1. Remain calm. This is important, as 82% of all victims panic within the first second of having their tongue stuck. The panic causes sudden movements and may

lead to ripping a layer of skin off your tongue. (Note: It is very amusing, once the pain subsides, to see your flesh frozen to a pole, but it's also very painful and is not recommended by Stats Canada.)

2. Be sure to ask a friend to "snap a pic" of this very Canadian moment. That picture will be sure to make you laugh at least once per year for the rest of your life. You're making memories here.

3. Remove your emergency hot cocoa from your coat pocket (it is statistically likely you are among the 91% of Canadians who carry a spare Thermos of hot cocoa on their person during the winter season). Pour the hot cocoa on your tongue. Be sure to get some in your mouth as well; there is no sense in wasting perfectly good hot cocoa.

4. Sing "O Canada" en français; this is commonly known to dry up the salivary glands and release the tongue. Since French-Canadian mouths work three times harder to get out half the amount of information, they tend to dry up quicker than those of the average English-speaking Canadian. Unfortunately, only 4% of anglophone Canadians can successfully get through the French version of "O Canada."

5. Have your friends attract a pack of timberwolves from the closest wooded area. The sight of hungry wolves is 440% scarier than the idea of ripping your tongue from a frozen pole. As soon as you see these wolves coming in for the kill, you will not think twice about yanking your tongue free and escaping the certainty of death. Stats Canada suggests the best way to attract the wolves is to post flyers reading, "Free Dinner: Wolves Only."

Follow these suggestions and Stats Canada projects you have a 12% chance of surviving this harrowing situation. Good luck.

Major Canadian
Weather Events

Because of its situation high in the northern hemisphere and its
exposure to three brutal oceans, Canada is truly at the mercy
of Mother Nature. While Canadians are used to dealing with all
manner of inclement weather, a few significant weather events
loom larger in the nation's meteorological memory.

Hurricane Becky: Eastern Canada, 1992
The Maritime provinces suffered a direct blow from a powerful
Category 5 hurricane, which destroyed hundreds of boathouses
and caused more than $7,000 in damage across the region.

"That Big Storm": Southern Ontario, 1999
The entire city of Toronto, Canada's undisputed economic
capital and vibrant cultural epicentre, was forced to an
uncharacteristic halt under the weight of nearly 20 cm of snow.
While it would have melted harmlessly within a few days, the risk
to Canada's identity was too grave. The full force of the military
was dispatched to dig the shivering bankers and theatre critics
out from their snowbound homes.

The Long Rain: British Columbia, 1982–1985

While the west coast receives its share of week-long rainstorms during any given year, few BC residents will forget the freak thunderstorm that actually lasted more than one thousand days. For three years the sun was a distant memory while nearly a kilometre of accumulated rainfall soaked the Vancouver area. This weather event is perhaps most notorious for sparking the Overcast Riot of June 1985.

The Assiniboia Tornado Event: Saskatchewan, 1960

Tornadoes are fairly rare on the Canadian prairies, but twisters have caused their share of damage over the years. Reports from one terrible day in 1960 indicate that at least a dozen unconfirmed twisters touched down across the province, disrupting literally tens of curling tournaments.

The Storm of the *Edmund Fitzgerald*: Lake Superior, 1975

When the waves of November come early, Superior can resemble an angry ocean more than the freshwater lake it is. On that fateful day, the crew of the *Edmund Fitzgerald* ignored Chippewa legends and weather reports equally, sailing straight into disaster—and AM radio immortality.

"Sandstorm": *Electric Circus*, 2000

They played this stupid song every gosh darn week that year. What a disaster.

Fashion

Dressing for Canadian Weather

If you're a Canadian hairless animal (e.g., Maple Leaf chicken breast) or a bald Canadian you know that the weather in Canada can be cold and unforgiving. An average Canadian winter consists of 304 days of complete darkness and roughly 3 million centimetres of snow nationwide. 96% of Canadians own at least one body tuque (jacket), and every Canadian knows that winter means for seven months you will be dressed like a doughy, undesirable mess and it's unavoidable. We're not here to tell you how to dress, but if you don't follow our guidelines you will perish.

Case Study: Churchill, Manitoba

In Churchill, Manitoba, 76% of the residents are polar bears. For the other 24% winter is especially harsh, and many human Manitobans will fall victim to polar bear bites, polar bear hugs, and exposure. To survive the harsh temperatures in Churchill, one can undergo a highly experimental surgery to become a polar bear. Currently, no other solutions exist for keeping warm in Churchill, Manitoba.

Case Study: Toronto, Ontario

Torontonians are notorious for dressing poorly during the winter months. For example, Becky hates wearing boots and thinks her jacket makes her look fat. "Longjohns under my skinny jeans? You're not even my real mom!" Becky is one of many Torontonians who believe that winter in Canada is an inconvenience to their wardrobe and will wear running shoes and ignore the unsavoury feeling of a drenched sock until the fourteenth or fifteenth snowfall of the season.

Torontonians traditionally brave through the seasons in the name of fashion, avoiding winter at all costs. Some typical behaviours include fleeing to mobile bunkers known as subways, moving about exclusively using the underground PATH system, or simply never leaving their expensive downtown condos.

Quick Tips

- One word: pelts. Two words: lots of pelts.

- Do not leave the house if you do not own a body tuque.

- Do not leave the house.

- Do not move to Salmon Arm.*

*Originally we assumed Salmon Arm had temperate weather conditions, but upon further investigation it appears they are currently buried under metres of snow.

- Buy a coffee; use the coffee to warm your hands during your commute. When you arrive at your destination, dump the cold coffee.
- Use Red Olympic Mittens for socks

Did You Know?

Canada has 27% more snow blowers than all other nations on earth combined.

What Are Canadians Wearing?

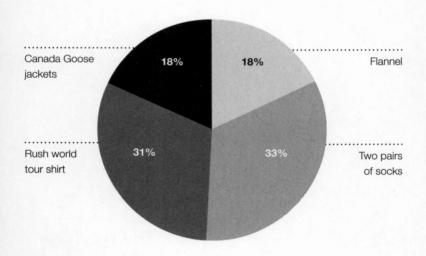

Canada Goose jackets — 18%

Flannel — 18%

Rush world tour shirt — 31%

Two pairs of socks — 33%

Canadian Fashion Trends

Fashion in Canada is dictated somewhat by the environment. Practicality trumps style most of the time. Still, Canada has created its share of fashion crazes. Here are the five most influential:

1830s—"The Trapper Trend": When the exploits of the coureur des bois reached the upper classes of European cities, many began copying the attire of these rugged fur traders. This was immortalized in the classic Gordon Lightfoot song "Coonskin Dandy."

1920s—"Mountie Madness": The surprise success of the film *O'Malley of the Mounted* spurred an intense fascination with RCMP attire on both sides of the border, with young men and women donning the traditional hats and jackets of the frontier force. The Mountie craze persisted for decades but ended abruptly after the series debut of *Due South*.

1960s—"Gump Gut": Young men and boys, inspired by the significant paunch of Montreal Canadiens goalie Gump Worsley, deliberately let themselves go to emulate their hero netminder. Chiselled abs disappeared from television and magazines, and stocky fatsos briefly became sex symbols across the land.

1980s—"Degrassi Diversity": The effect that *Degrassi Junior High* had on Canadian society cannot be overstated. One of the best examples of how the TV program indelibly influenced Canadian culture is the late-1980s trend of understanding and acceptance. It suddenly became fashionable for every young Canadian to be seen with a diverse and varied clique of friends, each with a set of easily relatable teenage problems. Thankfully, cynicism returned with the dawn of the 1990s.

1990s—"Snow Blindness": The worldwide "white reggae" phenomenon that defined the 1990s began when Snow released the enduring and unforgettable "Informer." Soon, men and women everywhere were wearing tracksuits and peering over wire-rimmed glasses. This uniquely Canadian contribution to global culture has proven to be our longest lasting; Canadian athletes competing in the 2010 Winter Olympics wore uniforms inspired by a certain Super Notorious Outrageous Whiteboy's style.

Flannel

Although the exact origins are unclear, flannel has traces in Wales, Germany, France, Ireland, Scotland, and England—this pedigree is very similar to that of many Canadian people, who when asked "Where are you from?" (roughly translated into, "What is your ethnic background?") will answer, "I'm a little Welsh, German, French, Irish, and Scottish, but mostly English." Sharing such an ambiguous and mixed history with flannel is the reason why Canadians have adopted it as their fabric of choice.

While flannel is technically a fabric, in Canada it is also a colour and a pattern. In fact, each family in Canada has its own unique flannel pattern—much like Scotland's tartans. The height of flannel's popularity came in the early days of Canada. Many Canadians worked in the outdoor trades like fishing, hunting, mining, and lumbering. Although all of these workers used flannel, it was primarily the lumberjacks who brought flannel into the mainstream culture. The durability, breathability, and warmth of the fabric was ideal for the woodsmen, who spent all day outside chopping trees. The term "rustic chic" was coined after these men made flannel look so good. Their broad shoulders and wide chests filled out the criss-crosses in a way that really made the patterns pop. Soon every Canadian had at least one flannel shirt in their wardrobe, but daywear wasn't enough. Canadians needed flannel at all hours. Pajamas were now flannel—Canadians loved flannel so much, they literally had to sleep in it. Flannel was now the primary colour, pattern, and fabric in Canada. During this period, when Canadians were asked what their favourite colour was 67% responded "flannel." Flannel and Canada were synonymous.

The pattern did experience an era of decreased popularity, though it never disappeared completely. People just weren't as into it as they once were. The early to mid-1990s saw a major resurgence in flannel's popularity. The grunge craze that originated in the Vancouver-adjacent town of Seattle swept Canada as well. Canadians quickly adopted this Generation-X-defining movement not because of the in-your-face music, or the I-don't-care attitude, but because of flannel itself. Canadians were once again excited to embrace the fashion of their forefathers/mothers and not be thought of as backwoods hillbillies. Flannel has returned to the height of its popularity in Canada—whether you are walking down the streets of Toronto or hiking through the wilds of British Columbia you are sure to come across someone wearing flannel, and wearing it proudly.

Plaid Distribution by Population

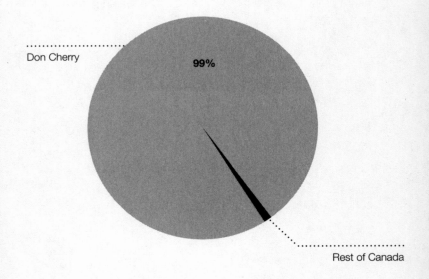

Don Cherry

99%

Rest of Canada

The Canadian Tuxedo
Deconstructed

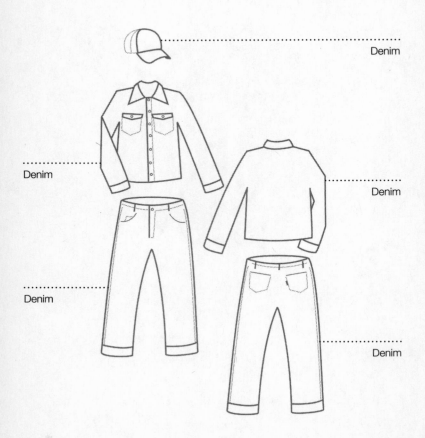

Denim

Denim

Denim

Denim

Denim

Famous Canadian Moustaches

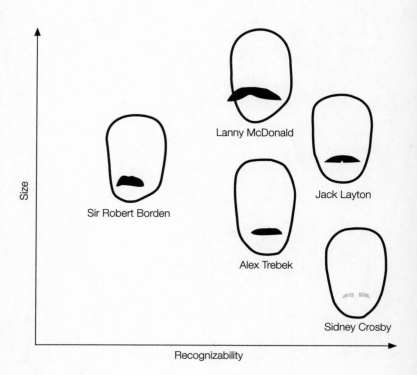

Lanny McDonald

Sir Robert Borden

Jack Layton

Alex Trebek

Sidney Crosby

Size

Recognizability

How to Dress for 10°C

January

April

July

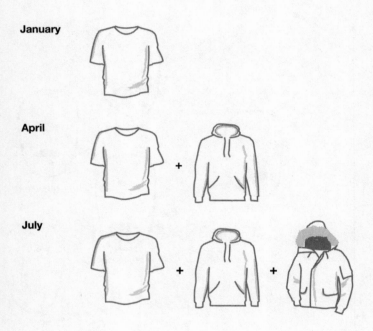

Arts AND Entertainment

The Spirit of Radio

Radio has a long and storied history in the formation of Canada. Radio waves travelled across the sparsely populated plains far faster than the horse and carriage ever could. Although most stations heard in Canada were from the US and Mexico, listening to them nonetheless gave the people a shared sense of moral superiority.

In the early days radio was an unregulated medium, which led to many unscrupulous businesses using popular music of the time to sell their dubious wares. For example,

"Oh Brother Where Art Thou Shoes From?" — The Discount
   Shoe Boys
"Sweet Mississippi Mash Liquor" — The Local Liquor Boys
"Holler at Your Mother's Cooking" — The Arbys Boys
"Thrifty Deals (With the Devil)" — The Salvation Army Boys

Modern radio call signs in Canada are made up of four letters, beginning with the two-letter combinations of CF, CH, CI, CJ, or CK.

These letter codes help categorize the content of each respective station. For instance:

- CF = Canadian Fun (lighthearted, whimsical content targeted toward free spirits)
- CH = Canadian Healthcare (dry, no-nonsense facts about living, breathing Canadians)
- CI = Canadian Ingenuity (cool gadgets and ideas, targeted toward aspiring inspirers)
- CJ = Canadian Judges (profiles of the Chief Magistrates, plus news of wacky verdicts from around the country)
- CK = Creepy Kanada

Canadian content laws have shaped the airwaves from province to province in a way that few Canadians understand. Law dictates that 25% of all songs and scripts on Canadian radio be produced by Canadians. This of course explains the popularity of Kim Mitchell and Avril Lavigne's ex-husband, but most Canadian Content (CanCon) stems from the lax requirements:

- 30% of your band is Canadian
- At least one member of your entourage has been to New Brunswick
- High mandolin content
- Written permission from Gord
- Live within 1,000 km of a Canadian border
- Name seems sorta French

Many believe that radio doesn't have a future in the age of Internet and podcasts, but still Canadian radio perseveres with new and exciting programming for a modern world. It helps that Canada has no movie or television industry to divert talented entertainers from the radio. Many famous Canadians got their start in radio, such as Rick the Temp, Barenaked Ladies, and Stephen Harper. These groundbreaking individuals represent the future of Canada, and would never have reached such heights without the magic of the airwaves.

CanCon Regulations

Canada lives in the cultural shadow of its powerful southern neighbour. The world's longest undefended border does little to stop the flow of movies, television, music, and Internet memes into Canadian territory. With that in mind, the Canadian Radio-television and Telecommunications Commission was formed in 1968 to establish a set of guidelines and quotas that help ensure Canadian culture is seen and heard.

Film Quotas

- 50% of New Yorks must actually be Toronto

- Every male actor's dialogue must be overdubbed by Jim Carrey

- Every successful spy movie parody franchise must be followed up with a perplexing critical and box office failure

Television Quotas

- Every third song performed on singing competitions must be "(Everything I Do) I Do It For You"

- A fish-out-of-water Mountie must be digitally inserted into every hard-boiled detective show

- Get ready for an awful Tim Hortons commercial like every six minutes

Music Quotas

- Every new artist must beat Rush at a battle of the bands

- Songs about boats are highly encouraged

- You can rap, but nothing filthy okay kids?

Facebook Quotas

- You must post the lyrics to "O Canada" to your timeline first thing each morning

- All friend requests must be accepted, and you must send a "thank you" for every like received

- Late-night messages to ex-girlfriends must be sent in both official languages

Canadian Women in Music

Canada has long been the home of a rich and vibrant music scene, and many of the most successful homegrown artists are women. You know them by their first names: Shania, Céline, Alanis, and so many more. Over the decades these women have been making music, Stats Canada has tracked their success and collected informative statistics to share with the country.

Shania Twain

- Sales of denim vests skyrocketed by 200% in 1995 thanks to Canadian moms wanting to look like Shania in the "Any Man of Mine" video.

- 16% of Timmins, Ontario's economy depends on the sale of coffee mugs with Shania's face on them.

- The average Canadian man became 77% less impressive after the release of Shania's third album.

Céline Dion

- 58% of Canadians believe that "cheese curds" is Céline's middle name.

- Repeated exposure to "My Heart Will Go On" is only 15% less miserable than drowning in the North Atlantic Ocean.

- Canadian dogs respond 73% more favourably to Céline's singing than do Canadian humans.

Alanis Morissette

- 34% of Canadians still cannot believe she was engaged to Ryan Reynolds.

- 86% of Canadians understand irony better than Alanis.

- Collectively, Canadian used-CD stores have enough unwanted copies of *Jagged Little Pill* for every living human on the planet.

Avril Lavigne

- Avril Lavigne's wardrobe is 45% ties.

- Avril Lavigne's marriage to Chad Kroeger is statistically the grossest in Canada.

- Avril Lavigne uses 87% of all the mascara in Canada.

Jann Arden

- 3% of Canadians think Jann Arden looks like their aunt.

- 23% of Canadians thought the guy who gave them the Jann Arden tickets said "Olive Garden gift certificates."

- 15% of Canadians do recall seeing Jann Arden on an episode of the *Rick Mercer Report* but that's it.

k.d. lang

- k.d. lang is the 14th most famous lesbian Albertan vegan country singer.

- k.d. lang is Canada's largest freestanding bowl of Kraft Dinner.

- k.d. lang missed every elementary school lesson on capital letters.

Sarah McLachlan

- Sarah McLachlan is Canada's most famous dog hoarder.

- 58% of Canadian pets are scared of Sarah McLachlan.

- Sarah McLachlan is the only Canadian artist who has not been nominated for a Juno.

Chantal Kreviazuk

- 99% of Canadians reading that name just said "Who?" (the other 1% was Raine Maida).

- Chantal Kreviazuk holds the record in Winnipeg for "most racially ambiguous name."

- Chantal Kreviazuk owns zero Our Lady Peace albums.

Did You Know?

In 1995, 78% of all exposed midriffs were Shania Twain's.

Rejected *Just for Laughs* Gags

According to a 2010 focus group conducted by Stats Canada, the most offensive and least funny *Just for Laughs: Gags* segments were as follows:

- Convincing your significant other that you're a ghost
- Calling your mother and telling her that her aunt Ruth has died
- Crying in a boat
- Telling your coworkers you were raised by a family of lobsters
- Wearing clothing that is three sizes too small and going to the local shopping centre
- Pretending to break wind in the middle of an important business meeting
- Dressing like a mime but then speaking to people

- Hugging expectant mothers

- Pretending the poutine you're eating is too hot

- Calling in bomb threats to Loblaws

- Eating candy in front of your diabetic grandmother

- Putting capers in your boss's salad

- Leaving an alligator in an elevator

- Pretending to like living in Montreal

- Filling someone's pockets with marbles and running away

Did You Know?

Canada's highest-rated TV show is "The Weather."

What Did Barenaked Ladies Buy with Their $1,000,000?

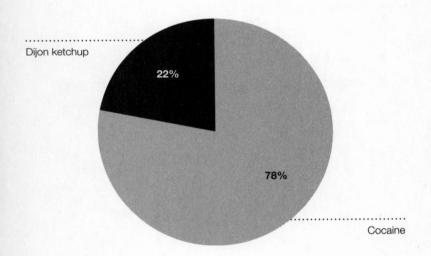

Dijon ketchup

22%

78%

Cocaine

Lesser-Known Canadian Pop Stars

The world is familiar with some of Canada's biggest pop stars.
But for every Bublé or Bieber or Barenaked Lady, you have a
thousand others who just never reached the same levels of
fame. The following are all Juno-nominated Canadian pop stars
who, although huge on MuchMusic, never became mainstream
successes on MTV.

- Jean McGuff—"Pass the Dutchie (Donut) on the Left Hand
  Side"

- Rita Gomesh—"(Your Heart Is) Colder Than the Prairies"

- Ben Mulroney—"Us Loonies Should Become a Toonie"

- Margot O'Shea—"Is That a Hockey Stick or Are You Glad
  to See Me?"

- Jessie and Tiffany—"We Found Love in a Tim Hortons
  Bathroom"

- Ryan Gosling—"Disney Is the Best"

- Lola Scotia—"(Fishing) for Love"

- Kelly Gruber—"Third Base"

- Paul-Jean Martinne—"Fries, Cheese & Gravy"

- Jimmy T.—"Keep Your Stick on the Ice"

- Julie NewMarket—"Today We Till the Soil"

- Henry LaFlamme—"The Belle of Laval"

- Ernie Wallace—"A Single Sip of Beer"

- Master T—"Welcome to Rap City"

- Bob—"Avec You"

- The Mounties—"You Can Stand Close If You'd Like"

- Gord Bauer—"Five Minutes for Heavy Petting"

- Fefe Subain—"Long Nights, Long Underwear"

- Brad—"Snow Job"

Howie Mandel vs. The Flu

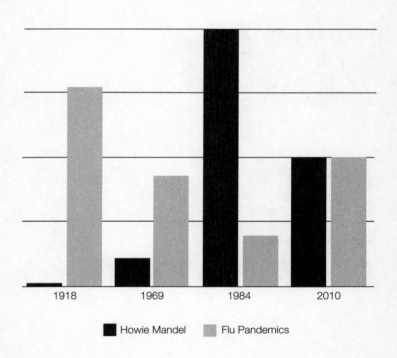

1918   1969   1984   2010

■ Howie Mandel   ■ Flu Pandemics

Stats Canada Spelling Bee: George Stroumboulopoulos

How to pronounce

jawrj strom-bohl-ah-poh-lis

Language of origin

Greek

Definition

A Canadian television icon known for his piercings, straight talk, and badassery.

Usage in a sentence

85% of Canadians "would pay good money" to kiss George Stroumboulopoulos on the mouth.

A helpful acronym to remember the correct spelling:

S even

T rusty

R CMP

O fficers

U sed to

M eet in

B arrie

O ntario

U ntil

L adies

O f

P eterborough

O ntario

U sed

L axatives

O n their

S teeds

Least-Popular CBC Spinoffs

According to a survey conducted in 2011, the least-popular CBC television spinoffs are as follows:

- *Doug the Beaver Hunter*
- *Heartland: Labrador*
- *Gord and Bob's Great Canadian Fish-off*
- *American Idol Canada*
- *So You Think You Can Dance, Eh?*
- *The Bachelor: Snowbirds*
- *The Bachelor: Walter Gretzky*
- *Walter Gretzky Variety Hour*
- *CSI: Salmon Arm*
- *Canada's Worst Goitre*
- *Acadian Idol*
- *RCMP Red*
- *Lake Boss*
- *Corner Gas 2*

Canadian Television Ratings

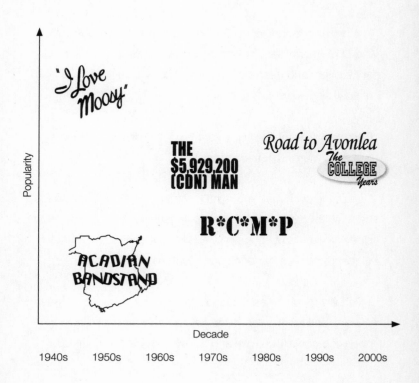

Canada's Walk of Fame

The words "Canadian" and "celebrity" are synonymous, much like Sharon and Lois, or Lois and Bram, or Bram and Sharon, or Elephant and a tambourine. If you can make it here, you can make it Anywhere.[1]

Canada's Walk of Fame is much like the Hollywood version, but has 90% more walk than fame.

Due to the overwhelming number of famous people in Canada, the Walk of Fame was created to let fans gawk at a name in the sidewalk instead of bugging Canadian celebrities when they are at their other job: bartending at Montana's Steakhouse.

To qualify for a star on Canada's Walk of Fame, an actor must have appeared in at least one *Law & Order* episode (in a speaking or walk-on role) and a Tim Hortons commercial; a

---

1 Anywhere is the name of a sparsely populated city in northern Saskatchewan.

musician must have one song featured in the opening credits of an American sitcom. Anyone else is chosen at random from a lottery.

Out of the 143 current inductees, 5% actually know where the Walk of Fame is located. The only celebrity to visit their own star thus far has been Kim Cattrall, who wanted to feel relevant again.

On average, 325 toes are stubbed annually on Nelly Furtado's star. This causes her record sales to skyrocket by .02%.

Pamela Anderson is the only celebrity to have two stars. They used to be placed tightly beside each other, but over the years they have shifted and cracked and are no longer a popular attraction.

The most overheard phrases at the Walk of Fame:

- "I just stepped in gum."
- "Hahaha, Burton Cummings. Get it? Get it?"
- "Take a picture of Nickelback's star. Just kidding. Let's get some fro-yo!"

- "There's a homeless guy asleep on Brendan Fraser's star. Nope, that's actually Brendan Fraser."

- "I can't believe I'm here! No really, why are we here?"

The Walk of Fame is a permanent reminder of how great Canada is as a nation, how proud we are of our hard-working citizens, and how you're only kind of somebody when America loves you.

Did You Know?

100% of Canadians know the names of every Canadian who's famous in the United States.

Fans of Justin Bieber

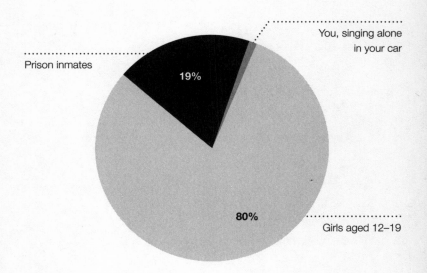

Prison inmates

19%

You, singing alone
in your car

80%

Girls aged 12–19

Top Ten Babes of All Time

According to a survey conducted in 2011, the biggest babes in Canadian history are as follows:

1. Mike Myers

2. Nellie McClung

3. Anne Murray

4. Roberta Bondar

5. Anne of Green Gables

6. Marie-Marguerite d'Youville

7. Lucy Maud Montgomery

8. Céline Dion

9. Alice Munro

10. Pamela Anderson

Sports AND Leisure

Hockey: A Canadian Game

Hockey is to Canada as long-distance running is to Kenya, being neutral is to Switzerland, and being fat is to America. It was invented to prove to other countries that we not only understand why water freezes but also can do something neat with it.

The first hockey skate was invented by accident in the mid-1800s when an Inuit man, whose feet had frozen in the subarctic temperatures, just wanted to feel something again so he stabbed himself in the feet with two double-sided blades. After sliding across the icy tundra with ease, he knew he was onto something. After he recovered from the blood loss, he attached the blades to boots and created transportation across the frozen lakes of the north.

95% of the Canadian population plays hockey (the other 5% don't have legs). Women have been allowed to play hockey only since 1998, after a vote of 155:153 in the federal House of Commons. Sarah "Nellie McClung" Thompson had been campaigning for years for this, and at the age of 67 played her first real game of hockey, breaking only three bones in the process.

85% of Canadian males "could have totally made it into the NHL." Most missed the draft due to knee injuries, lack of interest, or needy girlfriends.

134,234 Canadian babies were conceived after Canada won the gold medal in Men's Hockey at the 2010 Winter Olympics. Scientists have proven that Canadian men are more aroused by their favourite player scoring a goal than by their own wives, so children tend to be born 9 months after any championship. No babies have been born in Toronto since 1967.

Saskatchewan had an NHL hockey team from 1982–1983 called the Saskatoon Firehawks. They were accidentally left off the schedule for the next season and were too polite to say anything.

Wayne Gretzky not only was Canada's most well-known hockey player, but he also was premier of Alberta from 1986–1990 under the name Dwayne Grutzkii. Since Canadian premiers don't really do anything, no one seemed to notice.

The tooth count of the entire Vancouver Canucks team is 27. Reconstructive dentist is the third most lucrative profession in Canada, after beaver pelter and oil sands tycoon.

Did You Know?

88% of Canadians have a photo of themselves posing with the Stanley Cup.

Canadian NHL Team Profiles

Toronto Maple Leafs

- The average fan owns, at any given time, $3,000 in merchandise

- In 1992, inspired a 200% spike in baby boys named Wendel

- Has the average fan convinced the team is "just two good players" away from serious contention

- Plans a Stanley Cup parade every year

- 91% of fans cannot afford to attend a home game

Montreal Canadiens

- Every fan has rioted at least once

- 75% of cheers are boos

- Fans collectively consume 400 megalitres of Pepsi per home game

Edmonton Oilers

- 55% of fans wish they lived in Calgary instead

- Fans go to the arena because it's warmer than their homes

- 75% of fan time is spent gazing wistfully at the rafters, daydreaming of championships past

- Only arena parking lot in league designed to accommodate 17,000 pickup trucks per game

Calgary Flames

- 55% of fans wish they lived in Edmonton instead

- 78% of jerseys at home games still say Iginla

- Entire team never shows up to a game without a cowboy hat

- 60% of Calgary dads still sport a Lanny McDonald tribute moustache

Ottawa Senators

- Leafs fans make up 73% of the crowd for every game

- Only crowd in the league that does The Wave in both official languages

- 75% of fans wear official team-licensed dress shirts to every game

Vancouver Canucks

- 15% of fans can't make it through a game without wanting to throw a brick through the window of a Starbucks
- Team colours are blue and green to reflect the local environment (rain and mould)
- Are Canada's Stanley Cup–losingest team

Winnipeg Jets

- 45% of fans just want you to remember they have a team again
- Fans are loud so that people don't forget they are there
- Fans still can't say "Phoenix" without spitting on the ground
- Only arena parking lot in league equipped to handle plug-in block heaters for cars

The Playoff Beard: A History

The playoff beard is a staple of Canadian culture. However, our research suggests that the average Canadian is unaware of how the tradition began. We wanted to delve into the history of the playoff beard and provide a statistical analysis to give Canadians more information on the tradition that tickles us all.

For instance, while the average professional hockey player grows a beard for only a few weeks every season, bushy facial hair appears on more than 40% of all hockey cards. This unique Canadian tradition also leads to many unexpected injuries after the season has ended, as emergency room visits for razor burn peak geographically immediately after a local team is eliminated from the playoffs.

However, it's not all fun and games when it comes to this yearly ritual. One of the rarely mentioned reasons why Europeans didn't join the NHL until the '70s was that many fans felt their faintly coloured facial hair would be bad luck. It wasn't until Swede and eventual fan favourite Erik Eriksson joined the league with his bushy black beard that our whiskery friends from abroad were welcomed with open arms.

But what are the roots of this celebrated tradition? The history of the playoff hockey beard is a long and storied one. Canadians everywhere love the sight of a beard. The only thing Canadians love more than a full and bushy beard is hockey. Stats Canada would like to share the magical story of the fateful day when the two were combined.

It all began many years ago when one of the very first hockey players began to complain of his chin getting cold during games. Jimmy O'Shea played on the worst team in his amateur hockey league. They rarely won a game. To make matters worse for Jimmy, his face was always very cold. Playing on an outdoor rink will do that to you. When heavy drinking between periods did nothing to curb the chill, Jimmy started to grow a beard in the hopes that the whiskers would keep his face warm. Some hockey historians have described it as pure coincidence, but as Jimmy grew his beard his team began to win games. As his face got warmer his team got better. Jimmy's teammates drew a connection between their winning streak and his new beard, and they all began to grow beards in team solidarity. They found themselves playing in their league championship game. The entire team sported beards of varying fullness. Players on the opposing team were intimidated! They feared playing against these men who looked like they had just barrelled down from a mountain. Jimmy's team easily won the game, and the championship.

News of the team with the lucky beards travelled across Canada. Some laughed it off and called it chance. Regardless, players everywhere decided to give it a try. More and more grew hair on their faces in the hopes that it would propel their team to glory.

A tradition had begun.

Playoff Beard Statistics
- The team that has the player with the thickest beard has won the Stanley Cup 17 out of the last 20 seasons.
- The NHL playoffs account for 32% of lost revenue among Canadian razor blade companies.
- Food that gets lost in playoff beards is found only 2% of the time.
- 1% of every beer consumed by a hockey player is dribbled into his playoff beard.
- 68% of the country voted Sidney Crosby's playoff beard the worst of all time.

The Lucky Loonie

In 2002, both the men's and women's Canadian hockey teams won gold at the Winter Olympics in Salt Lake City. This event has gone down in history as "the drunkest Canada has ever collectively been."

Surprisingly, this national accomplishment wasn't because of skill or hard work, but because of the coin, now dubbed the "Lucky Loonie," that was placed under centre ice before the start of the tournament. (A copy of *Big Shiny Tunes 3* was the original choice, but was deemed too valuable.)

This coin now lives at the Hockey Hall of Fame in Toronto. It is touched more than 250,000 times a day by young and old alike, all of whom either are looking for a little luck or have a fetish for caressing the Queen's face.

The top 10 wishes made are as follows:

10. For *Corner Gas* to come back on the air.
9. One million more wishes (please and thank you).
8. For Avril to get married on Canada Day and ruin it for the rest of the country.
7. To become a MuchMusic VJ.
6. For Ryan Gosling and Rachel McAdams to finally work things out.
5. For [insert local sports team] to win [insert whatever trophy they would win].
4. To ride a Zamboni wearing nothing but a smile.
3. For Alanis Morissette to write a song about them.
2. For Justin Bieber to stop writing songs in general.
1. To not get some sort of cold or flu from touching this loonie.

Canadian Sports:
Toughness vs. Popularity

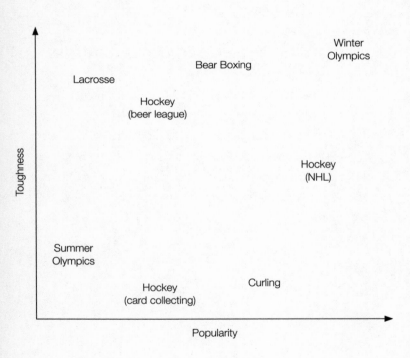

Lesser-Known Canadian Sports

According to a survey conducted by Stats Canada in 2012, the top 15 lesser-known but still important Canadian sports are as follows:

- Curling
- Loon calls
- Yelling obscenities from hockey stands
- Locating New Brunswick on a map
- Competitive apologizing
- Holding doors open
- Smile contest
- Maple syrup chugging
- Competitive handshaking
- Extreme ice fishing
- Frostbite wars
- Salmon wrestling (bears only)

- Singing the national anthem in French

- Completing a transaction using the French option at an ATM

- Cross-border shopping

 Did You Know?

The seven highest-paid athletes in Canada are all hockey mascots.

Canadian Football League: Rules of the Game

Number of Players per Team

The official number of players allowed on the field, per side, is 12. However, given the popularity of other sports that have the same season (hockey, curling, figure skating, etc.), it is very difficult to find a full team in Canada. Therefore, this is not a heavily enforced rule. As long as the team is willing to play, and there are not more than 12 players per side, the referee will allow the game to continue.

Field

A CFL field is 110 yards long, unlike the more typical field length of 100 yards. This is due to a calculation error when converting from imperial to metric and has no implications on the rules of the game. Canadian players still need to run the full 110 yards to score and not the 100 yards, no matter how politely they ask.

Game Play

Kickoff: Play begins when one team kicks the football to the other team from their 35-yard line. The player who receives the ball tries to run down the field to score a touchdown without getting hit. Tactics to avoid being hit include asking politely, crying, curling up into the fetal position, or tossing the ball away and asking your mom if you can quit football.

Rules of Contact: Football is a contact sport. Players throw their bodies at other players in the hope of knocking them down. In Canada, this is seen as impolite. Therefore, players must apologize and shake hands after each tackle is made.

Downs: Each team has three chances (downs) to advance 10 yards. If a team is unsuccessful in doing so the quarterback must walk the football to the opposing team's quarterback, hand it off, and wish him good luck.

Scoring: A team scores six points for a touchdown. A touchdown is when one team gets the ball into the opposing end zone. Celebrating and dancing are popular forms of gloating in the NFL. However, this is not the NFL. Canadian players will be penalized if caught "showing off" in any way. Only a simple wave of the hand or bow of the head is permissible, and players on both teams are encouraged (although not officially required) to applaud every touchdown.

The Toronto Huskies

Canadians are known for their pride in local sports teams. From the Cold War symbolism of the '72 Summit Series to the infamous Roughrider Riots, Canadians get behind their teams wholeheartedly. Even with all the storied Canadian sports franchises, the most beloved Canadian team of all time is, of course, the Toronto Huskies.

The Toronto Huskies existed for only one year, dominating the 1946–47 season of the Basketball Association of America. Fans across the country banded together in support of the only Canadian professional basketball team. All 60 Huskies games broke Canadian attendance records, with the exception of a two-week polio outbreak.

Proof of this exceptional year is that the Huskies hold several basketball records to this day:

- Most WWII Veterans on a Starting Lineup
- Warmest Uniforms

- Most Head Coaches in a Season
- Most Culturally Diverse
- Most Sexual Injuries

The Toronto Huskies also set the record for highest salaries in Canada, due to pressure applied by the Basketball Association of America. The Huskies soon became the wealthiest 1% in Canada. These unprecedented salaries led to many off-court antics, including daily parades, a pack of wild huskies, and of course, sexual debauchery: 1 in 5 Canadians is a direct descendant of a Husky.

The season was plagued with problems, including several trade disputes during a particularly nasty cold snap. Additionally, visiting teams constantly complained about the use of apple baskets for nets.

Free admission was given to any fans who were taller than George Nostrand, the tallest Husky at 6'8''. When Nostrand was traded mid-season the offer had to be applied to the next tallest Husky, who was 5'8''; ticket sales soon plummeted.

Over the course of their 60 games, the Toronto Huskies went through four head coaches, one of whom lasted only one game.

In all fairness, this was part of a fan promotion where anyone over 6'8" got to be head coach.

Despite a season of woes, the fans stuck with them. Men, women, and children alike would come out and cheer on their favourite players, even after their lone season was over. When the team dissolved in 1947, the remaining Huskies started playing against local high school teams and ragtag groups of weekend warriors. By 1960, they became known as the Brampton Globetrotters.

Canadians still fondly remember their cheer:

Here we go Huskies, Here we go!
Chew 'em up Huskies, Here we go!
When the other team scores, Bite 'em on the leg!
Rabid like a Husky, Here we go!

Canadian World Records

Longest beard: 152 cm—Jim Swanson, Whitehorse, YT

Most Timbits in one mouth: 64—Mark Duncans, Edmonton, AB

Largest hockey puck collection: 32,457.4—Steve Kingston, Toronto, ON

Smallest beaver: Squiggles, 1,300 g—Calgary Zoo

Longest hockey hair: 220 cm—also Jim Swanson, Whitehorse, YT (tied with the entire city of Nanton, AB)

Quickest execution of a double-double by a Tim Hortons employee: 2.3 seconds—Barbara Fisher, Winnipeg, MB

Most "sorrys" in a day: 45,125—Clara Quinn, Airdrie, AB

Greatest lake: Huron

Most overrated lake: Superior

Most hockey pucks in the face during one game: 6—
Patricia Walters, peewee hockey mom (wasn't paying attention)

Largest collection of pennies: The fountain outside of the Air
Canada Centre

Most time spent reliving the glory days: Don Cherry

Most patient: Ron MacLean

Little-Known Facts About 5-Pin Bowling

5-pin bowling was invented in Toronto in 1909 by Thomas F. Ryan at the Toronto Bowling Club. This remains Toronto's most significant contribution to the sporting world.

The 5-pin bowling ball is 1.47 kg, to be exact, or John A. Macdonald's birth weight (which is a little-known measurement used across Canada; for example, "I lost 2 JAMs this month").

The largest 5-pin bowling ball collection belongs to Reba Lovett, of Lloydminster, Alberta, with more than 3,000. Reba has never bowled a day in her life.

The number of pins was reduced from ten to five to make the game easier. This move also helped to ease the arthritis of Peter, the local whittler and pin-maker.

5-pin bowling is where Canadians get the motto, "If at first you don't succeed, try try again to a maximum of three times."

The tradition of wearing bowling shoes started in 1894, when Sir George Franklin, angry at his bowling loss, threw his shoes toward the pins where the ball return ate them. (The ball return at the time was a well-trained, but poor, 5-year-old boy.) Wanting to continue play, but not wanting to dirty his feet, he borrowed another man's footwear. When George was finished his game he returned the shoes, where they were then given to the next patron without any sanitation—a custom Canadians still follow today.

The cost of renting shoes can range from $3 for standard shoes to the $500,000 diamond-encrusted pair that is used exclusively by Howie Mandel at the Bowlerama in Etobicoke, ON.

A blue participation ribbon is given after every pointless frame.

When three strikes happen in three consecutive frames, it is called a "turkey." Traditionally, a live turkey is released into the building and the next player can't roll until it is found, killed, and plucked. In some cases it has taken the natural death of the turkey years later for the play to continue.

If a player's foot crosses the foul line, the pins knocked down in that frame are invalid. In American 10-pin, a loud buzzer sounds and everyone will know what you've done and why you are at fault, but in 5-pin, if you have a decent enough excuse or a doctor's note the infraction is overlooked and the game continues as is.

After 10 frames are played, the bowler with the highest score wins. In Canada, this involves a written congratulations from the prime minister and $25 in Canadian Tire money.

In 2009, a celebration of the 100th anniversary of 5-pin bowling took place at the brand-new Roll'n'Bowl in Burlington, ON. More than 30 people were in attendance! A photo of the creator's son, centenarian Thomas F. Ryan Jr., cutting the ribbon at the event now hangs in the Roll'n'Bowl right next to the men's washroom.

Canada at the Olympics

Canada might seem like an unlikely nation to aggressively pursue Olympic glory. Statistically, Canadians spend less time waving flags and shouting at foreigners than nearly any other people on Earth. Despite the fact that most sports tournaments in Canada end with all competitors "tied for first," Canadians have had a long and proud history at the Olympic Games.

When the first Olympiad was held in 776 BC, the land that would become Canada was still a young continent dotted by boiling volcanoes and scoured by retreating glaciers. By the time the celebration of sport and competition was revived in 1900, however, Canada had blossomed into a thriving colonial backwater.

The Canadian environment had made its people especially well suited to many of the events at that first modern Olympiad; a team of French-Canadian fur traders took gold in the rowing event, an Alberta rancher stunned the crowd by hog-tying the competition in the equestrian events, and a rowdy group of amateur shinny players from Cape Breton emerged on top of the cricket tournament. (It's specifically because of them that cross-checking was banned in cricket.)

Predictably, Canada has traditionally fared even better in the Winter Olympics, dominating events on the ice and the slopes. It's not uncommon to hear a Canadian athlete shout "Sorry!" when breaking from the pack and driving toward the finish line. In some winter sports, such as curling and ice fishing, Canada is often the only country to send any competitors at all.

Canada's three proudest moments on the Olympic stage have come as hosts. In 1976, Montreal welcomed the world to its state-of-the-art Olympic Stadium, although the opening ceremonies were somewhat marred by disaster when a huge chunk of concrete fell on the Venezuelan delegation. Canada apologized to the world by politely refusing to win a gold medal in any of the events held that year.

In 1988 it was Calgary's turn to host the Winter Games. Canada's athletes, grateful to be offered another opportunity to be at the centre of the Olympic spotlight, again refused to collect any golds. That act of athletic selflessness was overshadowed, however, by the heartwarming story of the Jamaican bobsled team. The attention given to their unsuccessful bid to blindly hurtle down an icy track inspired a generation of Canadian men and women to take up the sport, and today bobsled is the most popular winter activity in the nation.

Canada's defining moment in the Olympic spotlight came in 2010, when Vancouver was awarded the Winter Olympics despite the fact that it has the least-wintry climate in the country. This time Canada surprised the sporting world by reversing tradition and greedily collecting gold medals in heretofore unimagined numbers. The Canadian Olympic Committee's "Own the Podium" program was such a success that it spurred similar initiatives in other fields: Canadian scientists now aggressively pursue recognition via the "Nab That Nobel" program, and Canadian entertainers are encouraged to "Qualify for the People's Choice Award."

Perhaps the most important contribution the Olympics makes to Canadian daily life comes from the many sentimental, patriotism-baiting television commercials that become inescapable weeks before the games begin. This elaborate pandering to Canadian pride actually forms the basis of Canadian culture, defining the way Canadians see themselves and the coffee they drink. National pride increases nearly 60% during Olympic commercial breaks.

Due to climate change, it's expected that Canada will be the only country cold enough to host the Winter Olympics as soon as 2026. Even some smaller Canadian cities are preparing themselves for that eventuality, constructing new curling rinks and luge tracks in anticipation of the world arriving on their doorstep. Will Shawinigan, Wawa, or Wetaskiwin be able to deliver Olympic-sized highs and lows? If Canadian Olympic history is any indication—maybe!

 Did You Know?

87% of Canadian females own a Sidney Crosby body pillow.

Rejected Olympic Sports

The Canadian Olympic Committee has campaigned for the inclusion of many uniquely Canadian events over the years, but to date none have been accepted. We have compiled a list of some proposed and rejected Olympic events.

Icicle Fencing (1972)

Rhythmic Keg Stand (1980)

100 M Steriod Dash (1988)

0-Man Luge (1988)

Synchronized Jet-Ski (1992)

Pushing a Car
out of a Snowbank (1998)

Weightlifting (1996)

Freestyle Blogging (2004)

Desirability of Athletes by Sport

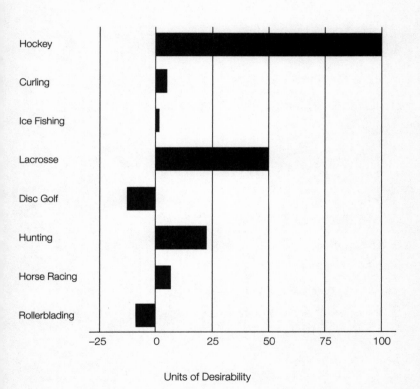

Units of Desirability

Rules for "Excuse Me, Sorry"—Canada's Favourite Board Game

Equipment

"Excuse Me, Sorry" game board

"Excuse Me, Sorry" card deck

16 "Excuse Me, Sorry" pawns (4 each blue, green, red, yellow)

Cold beer

Friends

Set-up

Shuffle the deck of "Excuse Me, Sorry" cards

Each player will arrange 4 of the same colour pawns at their corner of the board

Each player will express to the others that "it's only a game" and that they are "friends forever, bud"

Each player shakes hands with each other player; a playful pat on the back is optional

Objective

To be the first player to travel the complete game board with the fewest number of verbal or physical altercations with other players

Rules

Apologize when passing other players on the board

Move the appropriate number of spaces based on the card you choose

If you count the incorrect number of spaces you must immediately apologize to your friends

Do not deface or lose any cards

Be kind to one another

Have fun

Remember to bring a snack or 2-4 if playing at a friend's house

Do unto others

If at a friend's house, stay for a little while after the game and help clean up

Least-Popular Canadian Monopoly Pieces

According to a survey conducted in 2012, the least-popular Canadian Monopoly pieces are as follows:

Tim Hortons Grilled Panini

Inukshuk

Bust of Kim Campbell

Lock of Chad Kroeger's hair

Trillium flower

PC Decadent Cookie (real)

Lacrosse and You

Despite its official ranking as Canada's 47th most popular sport, lacrosse plays a significant role in every young Canadian's coming of age.

Compared to hockey, lacrosse does not stack up. Very few Canadians understand the rules of the game and even fewer care to learn. However, due to its status as Canada's national sport, the majority of middle and high school students are forced to play it during gym class. That many teenagers playing a contact sport together acts as a catalyst for awkward sexual experiences, arousing many questions about and interests in the human body. Four out of 10 Canadian boys get their first erection during a co-ed lacrosse game. Due to the overwhelming feelings that are awakened during the lacrosse unit, a 10-minute sexual education session is generally added at the end of class. The teacher (or coach) will randomly select and answer anonymous questions submitted into a shoebox.

Stats Canada has compiled these questions and ranked the top five as follows:

1. What is this feeling in my pants?
2. I have hair in weird places. Please explain.
3. Why do I sweat so much?
4. Will girls like me if I have a moustache?
5. Why can't I sing without sounding like a rooster?

In Quebec, lacrosse is called *le hockey joué à l'extérieur* because the word "lacrosse" has been appropriated as a slang term for masturbation, resulting in far too many giggles in gym class. Non-contact lacrosse is called intercrosse. This version has been tested in select schools across Canada but has only led to more sexual confusion.

Although lacrosse is ranked low in Canada in terms of popularity, its importance to sexual education is immeasurable and there are no plans to remove it from the education curriculum. The sport is integral to learning about one's sexuality and as such is fully supported by faculty and parents because it allows them to have the "birds and bees" conversation without being very direct about it.

Food AND Drink

Drinking in Canada

Drinking culture in Canada is primarily centred on sporting events. Simply watching awe-inspiring feats of athleticism is not entertaining enough on its own, so attendance at many spectator sports has become an excuse to drink heavily. Overpriced alcohol at sporting events represents a major part of the Canadian economy at 17% of Canada's GDP, second only to alcohol purchased for secret drinking.

Quick Facts

- All Canadian sports were invented under the influence of alcohol.

- Lacrosse started out as a way of launching fish at one's buddies.

- Basketball was born from a drunken prank involving hiding the neighbours' cabbages in hard-to-reach baskets.

- Curling began with sliding actual rocks into actual houses, particularly the houses of friends who refused to come out drinking.
- Hockey just doesn't make any sense.

Spectator sports are not the only excuse for drinking in Canada. Many of the most common everyday activities in Canada incorporate alcohol. In fact, for every Canadian calorie burned through exercise, an equal and offsetting calorie is added by alcohol. This keeps fitness levels in Canada exceptionally mediocre.

The most popular drinking sports in Canada are the following:

- Curling
- Softball
- Darts
- Ladies' Curling
- Fantasy Hockey
- Lawn Mowing
- Ultimate Fighting
- Soccer Momming

- Netflix Hunting
- Accidental Tobogganing

The drinking age in Canada is either 18 or 19, depending on the "cool factor" of each province. However, in Manitoba and Alberta, residents can legally drink at 16 if they have parental guidance. In the rest of Canada, residents can drink at 12, depending on the "cool factor" of their uncles. Since the drinking age in the United States is 21, this leads to the phenomenon known as CBBT (Cross-Border Booze Tourism). The economies of cities such as Windsor and Sault Ste. Marie are almost entirely dependent on CBBT; 85% of all hotel rooms in downtown Windsor are currently occupied by Michigan State fraternity brothers. While CBBT injects billions into the Canadian economy, an offsetting phenomenon occurs when Canadians turn 21 and realize that alcohol is incredibly inexpensive in the United States. Thanks to America's extravagant subsidies on empty calories, this balance has kept both countries' economies strong for generations. For further information on Cross-Border Booze Tourism, ask a weird border kid.

Drinking also has a profound effect on the Canadian economy in that it creates new secondary markets based on the value of empty bottles. At a rate of 5 cents a bottle (10 cents in Quebec),

Canadians have a significant portion of their wealth tied up in empties, not realizing their true value. Improperly discarded bottles are quickly reclaimed by the homeless and vagabond communities, who have turned them into a makeshift currency. Within each major city of Canada, a "Bottle King" arises atop this economy. All the Bottle Kings of Canada pay dues to "Le roi de bouteilles," who retains supreme power due to the higher value of bottles in Quebec. This phenomenon was immortalized in the classic Gordon Lightfoot song "Bottle King."

Drinking has a long history in Canada and is still a crucial part of everyday life. The presidents of Canadian beer companies are elected after a bruising five-week campaign. Public transit is free in Canada if you're drunk. Beer t-shirts clothe 85% of Canada's homeless. Studies have shown that, without alcohol, Canadian life would be exactly as boring as Americans think it is.

Canadian Drinking Game Statistics

Canadians love to drink, and drinking has become a part of the national culture. Occasionally, Canadians even drink to excess (shocking, we know) and when they do, they sometimes partake in games designed to increase their intake of alcohol. We've collected an assortment of statistics that help shed some light on the drinking habits of Canadians.

- 52% of Canadian drinking games result in streaking.
- 1 in 4 *Hockey Night in Canada* drinking games involve the participants chugging a beer whenever Don Cherry pronounces a player's name wrong.
- Every drinking game that occurs during a Royal Wedding involves bad British accents.
- 48% of drinking game participants will use Molson Canadian beer "if we can't find anything better."
- Drinking games are played during broadcasts of CBC shows to stave off sleep.

- Smirnoff Ice coolers are the most popular drink during *Degrassi*-inspired drinking games.

- 77% of Canadian drinking games are played to stay warm.

- In 1998, Canadians played a drinking game called "Take a Shot Every Time You Hear 'My Heart Will Go On' on the Radio," resulting in four deaths.

- The *Road to Avonlea* drinking game is most popular among Canadian women ages 47 to 62.

- When playing beer pong, 93% of Canadians use Tim Hortons cups.

DISCLAIMER: Stats Canada does not endorse drinking under the legal drinking age, and especially does not endorse driving to the provinces of Alberta, Manitoba, and Quebec if you are 18. We also don't endorse anyone drinking crappy beer. Spend that extra few dollars. It's worth it. We promise.

Canadian Cocktails

Few things are more Canadian than getting intoxicated. 87% of people reading this report are probably intoxicated right now! Stats Canada does not condone the overuse of alcohol, but if one must partake, here are the most Canadian drinks according to the 2011 Census.

The Puck Bunny

1 oz marshmallow vodka
64 oz arena beer
1 maple leaf
1 handful jersey lint
Pour over ice from a goalie
    crease

The Old Sled

1 part aged bourbon
1 part memories
A dash of rust
A push from your dad

The Canada Goose

3 oz Grey Goose Vodka
3 oz grey goose
1 oz Great Lakes water

The Bacon-eh-tor

1 part bacon-flavoured vodka
1 part bacon-flavoured water
1 part bacon
Pour into bacon-rimmed shot
    glass

The Mountie

8 oz dry gin

6 oz horse vermouth

98 oz a gun

The Rush Fan

12 oz white wine spritzer

1 glowing recommendation
    from Jian Ghomeshi

1 t-shirt from 1980, in
    excellent condition

1 heavily syncopated rhythm
    track

The Nanaimo Bar-Hopper

1 local, seasonal, artisanal
    pale ale

50 mL Pacific seawater

1 organic orca egg

Garnish with a sprig of cedar

The John A.

50 mL scotch

65 mL blended scotch

60 mL whiskey

55 mL whisky (no "e")

Canadian Food Pyramid

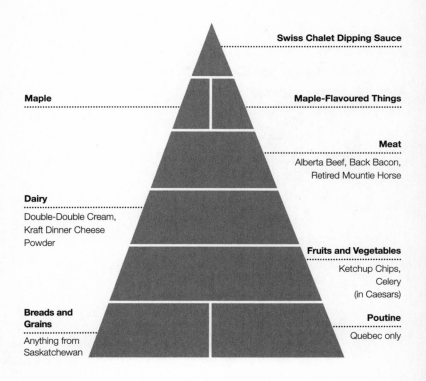

Swiss Chalet Dipping Sauce

Maple

Maple-Flavoured Things

Meat
Alberta Beef, Back Bacon,
Retired Mountie Horse

Dairy
Double-Double Cream,
Kraft Dinner Cheese
Powder

Fruits and Vegetables
Ketchup Chips,
Celery
(in Caesars)

**Breads and
Grains**
Anything from
Saskatchewan

Poutine
Quebec only

What's in a Double-Double?

60% Scalding Hot
100% Arabica Beans

20% Cream

20% Sugar

What Can You Win When You "Roll up the Rim"?

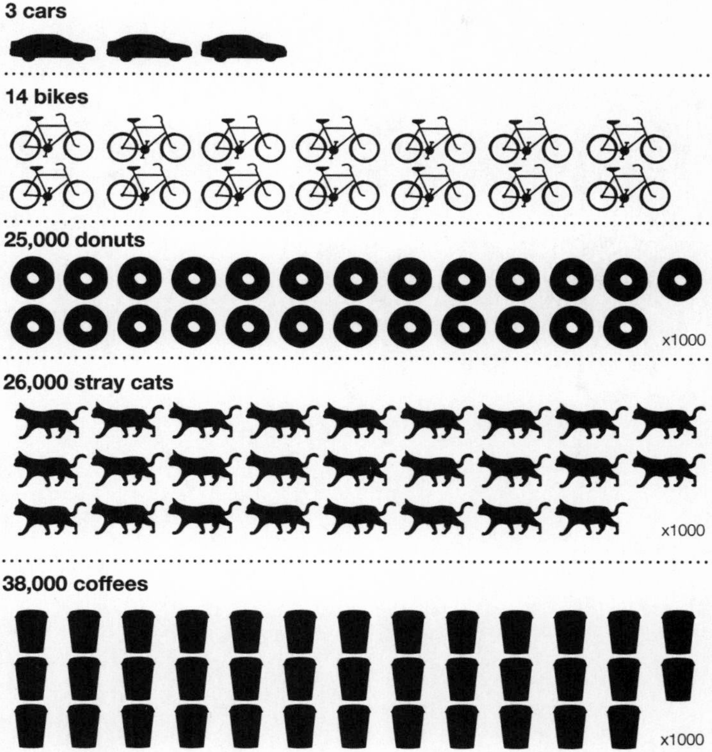

3 cars

14 bikes

25,000 donuts

x1000

26,000 stray cats

x1000

38,000 coffees

x1000

Most Popular Canadian Donuts

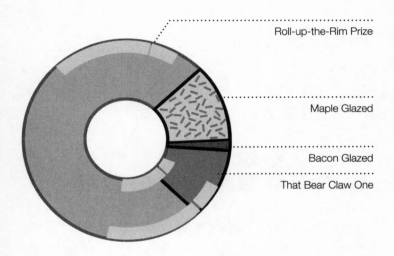

Roll-up-the-Rim Prize

Maple Glazed

Bacon Glazed

That Bear Claw One

What Kinds of Pies
Are Canadians Eating?

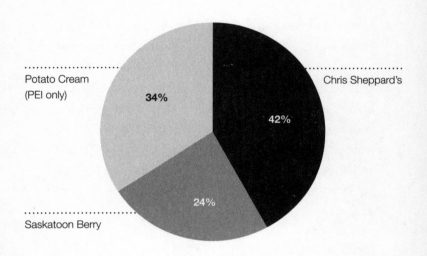

Potato Cream
(PEI only)

34%

Chris Sheppard's

42%

Saskatoon Berry

24%

A Brief History
of the Nanaimo Bar

This popular no-bake Canadian dessert was created in
Nanaimo, BC, in the early 1950s. Gas and electricity were
introduced to Vancouver Island only in 2003, so during that time
food could be either cooked over an open flame or not at all.
Mabel Jenkins, creator of the Nanaimo Bar, was given the Order
of Canada in 1974 for her achievements in "baking." She later
went on to date Gordon Lightfoot and was the inspiration for the
classic Gordon Lightfoot song "If You Could Read My Mind."

Popularity of the layers (in %)

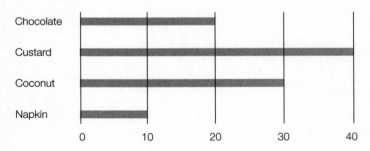

Other facts about the Nanaimo Bar:

- The bar is correctly pronounced "nay-nay-emo"

- The mascot "Nanaimo Bear" was banned from parades in 1997 for making a lewd gesture

- Locals call the dessert "those chocolate coconut things … you know, with the custard"

- Due to overwhelming popularity, a tray of the bars became mayor of the BC town from 1967–1972, until it was accidentally assassinated at a town hall meeting

- Creator Mabel Jenkins went on to create other no-bake desserts such as "whipped cream in a pie pan" and "orange slices"

- The American version, the "Akron Square" (which adds a layer of cheddar cheese), has not been as widely received

- Other failed innovations include the "Nanaimo Bar" (an actual bar) and the "Nanaimo Bra"

Sex AND Dating

Sex in Canada

Sex in Canada is much like sex in the rest of the world, but there are some peculiarities. Some have to do with the climate: the average Canadian striptease takes 12 extra minutes to perform. Others have more to do with culture: many Canadian women cannot conceive once their hockey team has been eliminated from the playoffs.

We at Stats Canada have carefully collected and analyzed data relating to the sex lives of Canadians. Here's a snapshot:

- Most Canadian men first learned the fundamentals of sex from that weird older guy on their bantam hockey team
- Residents of Climax, Saskatchewan, report the highest degree of satisfaction
- 65% of bears on Grindr Canada are actual bears
- In Alberta, reverse-cowgirls outnumber regular cowgirls 5:1

- Quickies are twice as likely to occur during "Satellite Hotstove" than during "Coach's Corner"
- Women and men both use the word "sexy" to describe Ryan Gosling in equal numbers

Canada's history is full of sexy moments: the Vikings brought more than long ships and sod houses to L'Anse aux Meadows; they also imported pragmatic Scandinavian sexual morality. Those early settlers of Newfoundland's northernmost tip started Canada's first nudist beach, although traditional Norse hats were still mandatory. (Etymology note: this is where we get the word "horny" from.)

However, the liberated views of the early 1000s were a fondly distant memory by the time French and English explorers reached the continent. A sexual dark age descended upon the icy land as its coastline and waterways were being tentatively probed by these overdressed agents of foreign kings and queens. Jacques Cartier and his men frequently found themselves lost, as they were too embarrassed to expose their sextants in public. By the time the Jesuits were fighting their way through the bush to bring religion and shame to the natives, sex was more myth than reality.

Canada's sexual winter lasted until a thaw finally came in the mid-20th century. The arrival of radio and TV allowed a more relaxed attitude toward sex to seep across from our southern neighbour. By the time Pierre Trudeau famously launched his bid for leadership of the Liberal Party from a Montreal swingers' club, Canada's sexual springtime was in full bloom.

Today, Canada is renowned as a top producer of global sex symbols:

- Pamela Anderson: actress, renowned breast-haver
- Ryan (Reynolds/Gosling): actor, setter of impossible abdominal standards
- Paulina Gretzky: hockey royalty, hot mess
- Chad Kroeger: singer, patron saint of sexually aggressive hillbillies
- Mary Pickford: silent film star, inventor of dirty talk
- Shania Twain: singer, popularizer of leopard-print attire for CMILFs

Our research indicates that Canadians have more sex than any other people on Earth. Theories as to why Canada is so sexy are numerous; it could be the opportunity afforded by endless winter nights, or the thrill of the short, steamy summers. It could be the "will-they-won't-they" tension of French/English relations. It could be the national passion for a sport where muscular men "grind it out," "shoot it hard," and "look for a hole." The mystery remains, but we here at Stats Canada will leave no HBC blanket unturned in our quest to quantify the sex lives of Canadians.

Did You Know?

Jarome Iginla has appeared in 126,000 sex dreams since his NHL debut.

Where Does Canadian Sex Happen?

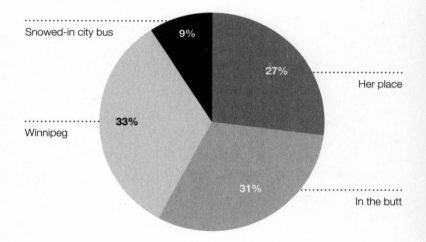

Snowed-in city bus

9%

27% Her place

33% Winnipeg

31% In the butt

Canadian Sex Positions

- The Lunenburg Lighthouse
- The Shawinigan Handshake
- The Rusty Zamboni
- The Hurry Hard
- The NAFTA (Canadian 69)
- The Salmon Arm
- The 4:30 Sunset
- The Big Nickel
- The Breaker High
- The Saskatchewan Roughrider
- The Ottawa Rough Rider
- The Garbage Strike
- The Dry Tugboat
- The Bi-Way
- The Sudbury Bypass

- The 100% Alberta Beef
- The Southernmost Tip
- The N-DP
- The Bluenose
- The Canadarm
- The Cremation of Sam McGee
- The Halifax Explosion
- The Corner Gas
- The Heritage Minute
- The Giant Tiger
- The Bruce Cockburn
- The Two-Man Skeleton
- The Thriving Beaver
- The Regina Inn
- The Dump and Chase
- The Midnight Sun
- The Mattawa Milk Bag
- The Moose Rack
- Sled-Doggy Style
- The 5-Hole

- The Franklin Expedition
- The Split the D
- The JFL Gags
- The Smoked Meat Sandwich
- The Group of Seven

Did You Know?

39% of carrots grown in Canada will become snowmen penises.

Canadian Pick-Up Lines

Through the public census, Stats Canada has found that 71% of all Canadian long-term relationships started while waiting in the returns line at the local Home Hardware. Although these relationships were founded on their romantic location, they would not have flourished without the initial pick-up line. In Canada, a pick-up line has a rate of effectiveness of one in four, which means that 75% of them will not yield desired results. Of the 25% that are successful the following (or a variation of) have an achievement rate of 90% or higher:

- Hey fella, is that a mini-stick in your pocket or are you just excited to see me?

- Girl, I've got two tickets to the Gordon Lightfoot concert and one of them has your name on it.

- Damn, your eyes are more beautiful than the aurora borealis in Dawson City during mid-fall.

- Baby, you've got my blood rushing faster than the waters of Niagara Falls—the Canadian side.

- Hey there big guy, you've got a body that would make a hard-working lumberjack jealous.

Therefore, if you are in the market for a potential life partner it is statistically sound to try out one of the pick-up lines listed above. If, however, you are unsuccessful, do not give up. Your chances of scoring (hockey reference) increase 4% for every attempt made.

Did You Know?

12% of Canadians have had a sexual fantasy involving Jean Chrétien's voice.

Canadian Singles

With the increase in popularity of the Internet, Canada has seen a proportionate rise in Internet dating. 80% of Canadian couples met online, whether they realize it or not. 70% of couples who meet online stay together an average of 15 years. 60% of these couples get a cat together.

The most popular online dating site is "Canadian Singles," with more than 7 million registered users and another 10 million who are "just looking."

cHarmony

The CN Tower
Sex: Male (duh)
Age: Late 30s
Location: Downtown

Eye Colour: Glassy
Hair Colour: Blinking lights
Height: 553 m
Weight: Pride of a nation
Body Type: Slim
Favourite Food: Prix fixe
Favourite Movie: *Sleepless in Seattle* (lolol)
About Me: I'm a little shy … I have season tickets for the Jays if you're into that … I did call the doctor after 4 hours but it hasn't gone down yet … haha just joking ;)
Turn-ons: Upscale dining, tourist season, tall people
Turn-offs: Wind, the Argos, those idiots hanging off the side
Ideal Date: BATHE IN MY MAJESTY

cHarmony

Messages   Matches   Provincial Park Info

Displaced Fisherman

Sex: Male
Age: 42
Location: Fort McMurray

Eye Colour: Steely
Hair Colour: Salmon blond, very oily
Height: Respectable
Weight: Respectable
Body Type: Fisherman
Favourite Food: Cod fries
Favourite Movie: *Jaws 4: The Revenge*
About Me: I just moved to Alberta from St. John's, looking for work, and maybe some play ... I love my three kids, my dog "Newf," and a cold beer after a hard day at work. I am so scared of Alberta.
Turn-ons: Life jackets, fertility, folksiness
Turn-offs: Oil, sand, forts
Ideal date: A three-week trip to Newfoundland

cHarmony

Messages   Matches   Provincial Park Info

The Loon
Sex: Female
Age: 12
Location: Muskoka

Eye Colour: Blood red
Hair Colour: Salt'n'pepper
Length: 76 cm
Weight: None of your beeswax!
Body Type: Athletic
Favourite Food: Sushi
Favourite Movie: *Free Willy*
About Me: Laid-back and looking for love! I'm a super chill aspiring singer/songwriter who loves a dip in the lake! Not looking for any one-night stands or flings, I'm ready for a partner who is willing to mate for life.
Turn-ons: Avid swimmer, fertile, shrill voice
Turn-offs: Land dwellers, poor swimmers, raccoons, weasels, skunks, lacklustre plumage
Ideal date: A weekend getaway to the cottage

cHarmony

Messages | Matches | Provincial Park Info

Mountie
Sex: Male
Age: 38
Location: The frontier

Eye Colour: Steely
Hair Colour: Covered by hat
Height: Imposing
Weight: 550 kg (with horse)
Body Type: Mountie
Favourite Food: Justice served cold
Favourite Movie: *Three Kings*
About Me: I just transferred divisions, single and ready to mingle. Not much crime out here, so it's pretty chill. I like to get loose, especially when off-duty. I want to meet somebody I have a spark with (but not like a taser lol).
Turn-ons: Damsels (distressed), the rule of law, chaps
Turn-offs: Saddle sores, criminality, smartphone cameras
Ideal Date: Brushing the burrs out of Rusty's mane, followed by a romantic musical ride under the unforgiving prairie sky

Canadian Turn-Ons by Age: Women

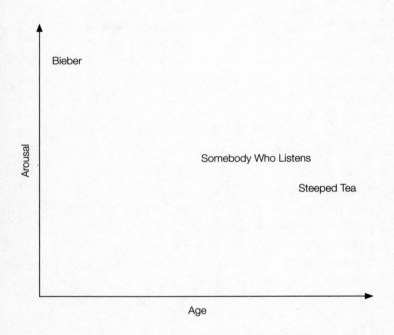

Canadian Turn-Ons by Age: Men

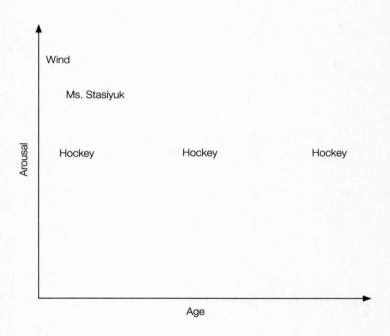

Kidz Korner

Kidz Korner: Did You Know?

Apparently, statistics and numbers are seen as "boring" and "nerdy" by 97% of all Canadians under the age of 13, who would rather build science dioramas and mix baking soda with vinegar. However, Stats Canada believes statistics and numbers are super cool, so we've decided to dedicate a section of our book to the youth of Canada, to hopefully draw them into the exciting world of statistics, trends, analyses, and equations.

Did You Know ...

- Canada's national groundhog, Wiarton Willie, is really just a man named Doug who lives underground for most of the year.

- The majority of Canadians just upgraded their computers to Windows 97.

- Sir John A. Macdonald invented Canada in 1878.

- Quebec is 1,542,000 km² of cheese curds.

- Pierre Elliott Trudeau "did it" with 8,694 Canadian women during his life.

- The rest of the Great Lakes do not like Lake Michigan.

- Canada's extensive forests are home to bears, deer, wolves, Céline Dion, beavers, birds, raccoons, and other such animals.

- The St. Lawrence River is the patron saint of beluga whales.

- Sir John A. Macdonald's blood alcohol level was at least 28% at all times.

- The most famous historical Canadian figure is a cartoon bear named Winnie-the-Pooh.

- James Naismith was exiled from Canada in 1892 for inventing the game of basketball.

- Canada became a country on July 1, 1867, when it finally approached British Parliament and said "please."

Colouring Book: Famous People Who Have Been to Canada

Queen Elizabeth

Ronald Reagan

Arnold Schwarzenegger

Oprah Winfrey

Questions to Stats Canada from Ms. Stasiyuk's Grade 3 Class

In another bid to foster an interest in statistics, Stats Canada reached out to an average Grade 3 class and asked them to send some questions about Canada for us to answer using our vast database of facts and figures.

Question: How many national parks are there in Canada?
Answer: The number of national parks in Canada is actually unknown. The north of Canada is mostly uninhabited and untravelled because of its barren land and frigid weather. It is almost impossible to know how many national parks could be up there.

Question: Do some people still live in igloos way up in the north?
Answer: No. The traditional igloo has disappeared from Canada's north, and few modern Inuit remember the traditional construction methods. Instead, entire subdivisions of nearly identical ice houses (each with a double-sled garage) have taken their place. Inuit teenagers hate it.

Question: Is there electricity in Labrador?

Answer: Yes, but everything is run on battery power. 97% of all Duracell sales in Canada occur in Labrador.

Question: Why are the prairies so flat?

Answer: Well, some provinces don't develop as quickly as other provinces. It's probably tough when your neighbouring province has already sprouted an alluring range of peaks, but Canada's beautiful, utilitarian prairies should just be patient and wait for plate tectonics to work their gradual magic.

Question: Why is Newfoundland and Labrador the fattest province in Canada?

Answer: Since the official provincial name change, the people of Newfoundland and Labrador spend 43% of their day articulating and spelling their province's name, leaving very little time and energy to prepare a well-rounded, healthy meal.

Question: How big is Canada?

Answer: Canada is big. In fact, it's the second-biggest country in the world—only Russia is larger. In all of Canada's class pictures, it's always in the back row.

Question: How old is Canada?

Answer: Canada was founded in 1867, but did not achieve full independence from Britain until 1982. Canada had to sit at the kids' table at the United Nations until 1999.

Question: How many Canadians are there?

Answer: At last count, there were more than 34 million Canadians. You are probably one of them, and so is hip-hop sensation Drake.

Question: What are the most populous provinces and territories?

Answer: It does not matter how many people live in a province. What matters is how "cool" each province is. The top five coolest provinces/territories are ranked, in order, as follows:

1. Ontario (duh)
2. Nova Scotia
3. Ontario
4. Prince Edward Island
5. Ontario

Note: The five least-cool provinces in Canada are all Quebec.

Kidz History:
Vimy Ridge Mad Lib

During the First World War, Canada, then home to barely
7 million people, was still very much a dominion of the British
Empire—so, when England was at war, Canada's (_adjective_)
army was also at war.

The Battle of Vimy Ridge was one of Canada's triumphs during
the First World War and one of the most meticulously planned
(holiday, plural). Vimy Ridge was then under German control and
had been since 1914. The task at hand was for France to regain
control of the (_cut of beef_) area.

After leaving the Somme, the Canadian soldiers studied this
area throughout the winter until they knew it like the back of their
(_favourite body part_). They built a replica Vimy Ridge and also
dug into No (_favourite gender_)'s Land in an effort to get as close
to enemy lines as possible.

On March 20, 1917, the Canadians began their (_adjective_)
assault and successfully weakened the German front lines.

On April 2 the Canadians increased their firepower, and on April 9 the Canadians attacked. The battle took place atop a (_body sound_) hill on April 9 to April 12, 1917, in the Nord-Pas-de-Calais region of France during a particularly harsh winter.

The Canadians eventually regained the area, which was something the British and French could not complete after (_rhymes with penny_) failed attempts.

The key strategist behind Vimy Ridge was Canadian officer and former (_animal_) Arthur Currie. Currie later became the commander of the Canadian army and continued to (_verb_) the Canadians for the duration of the war. Arthur Currie was later knighted for his efforts by King George (_favourite roman numeral_).

Out of the nearly 100,000 Canadians who fought at Vimy Ridge, 3,598 died and 10,602 were (_verb_). After the war, the Canadians were now known as more than just a dominion, but a (_colour_) force and a (_write down cool_) army. Canada was granted a (_small animal_) in the League of Nations in 1931.

Kidz Sports: Hockey Post-Game Interview Mad Lib

We've got to get out there and give it (*number larger than 100*) percent.

During the penalty kill, (*surname, with a y on the end*) made a great play. We thought that would (*verb*) things around.

We just need to remember that as long as you're takin' shots eventually you're gonna (*verb*).

We've gotta keep our (*noun, plural*) on the ice. Really doin' it to honour (*figure, fatherly*) out there.

The first (*period of time*) was strong. We came out with high energy. We were firing on all (*car part, plural*). We lost momentum, and we couldn't find a way to bounce back.

Our fans at home always make a lot of (*noun*), and that fires us up. If we're going to win these games we have to keep firing on all (*car part, plural*).

You know, there's 82 games. It's a tight (_noun_) for the playoffs.

We played a strong game last night in (_Canadian city with high unemployment_), but we need to be able to do that every (_religious holiday_).

Just gotta (_verb_) every shift.

We have (_number_) games left—we only need to win (_larger number_) of them.

When you come down to it, we couldn't put the (_round, flat object_) in the (_another word for net_).

Look, I've got three kids at home and I'm just so scared of getting hurt every time I step on the ice. I don't know how to do anything else, I'm not like my dad. This is my last shot.

Quiz: Which Coin Are You?

1. How would you describe your style?

   a. Feathered

   b. Furry and mostly brown

   c. Earthy

2. What element can you not live without?

   a. Water

   b. Water

   c. Water

3. What is your idea of the perfect date

   a. A weekend away at the cottage

   b. Starting a project like building a house

   c. A picnic in a heavily wooded area

4. Would you describe yourself as an animal?

   a. Yes

   b. Yes

   c. No

5. If you could live anywhere in the world, where would you live?

a. Muskoka

b. A damp woodland area

c. Algonquin Park

6. How would your friends describe you?

a. Beautiful, demon-red eyes with a voice that shatters glass

b. Portly, industrious, and clammy

c. A leaf

Mostly A's: You are the Loonie

Mostly B's: You are the Nickel

Mostly C's: You are the Penny

Conclusion

The book you just read was the product of decades of research and analysis, part of an unprecedented inquiry into the lives of Canadians from coast to coast. At Stats Canada we take our responsibility seriously, pledging a solemn oath to collect data carefully and without bias. Some will take issue with our findings, but be assured that we upheld the highest standards possible when conducting the research that went into this publication.

Expenses Incurred:

- Food & beverage: $420,000
- Transportation: $65,000
- Hockey tickets: $44,000
- Bear spray: $532
- Airport Wi-Fi: $111
- Canoe wax: $74.30
- Orange juice: $12
- *The Love Guru* Blu-Ray: $5

In many ways, our great nation defies conventional statistical analysis. Canadians are a complex and often contradictory people, but we have identified many things that weave the nation together like a brilliant flannel quilt. In every province and territory, Canadians can be found exercising their elbows at the bar, second-guessing the instincts of every NHL general manager. All citizens can rattle off an impressive list of Canadian celebrities on command, and every Canadian can argue convincingly that their home province is the prettiest (except for New Brunswick).

In addition to those perennial similarities, we also observed some significant changes compared to previous studies. Canadians everywhere are working longer hours, from the transplanted oil patch worker rising before the sun in Northern Alberta to the laid-off auto worker manning the overnight coffee shop drive-thru shift in Southern Ontario. Canadian families are shrinking, as parents opt to have fewer children in the face of rising education costs and Rogers bills. And while anglos and francophones continue to spar over government services and signage laws, the future of the country is being discussed in dialects neither group cares enough about to understand.

Over its short history, Canada has been in a state of constant evolution. One hundred years hence, will Canada resemble the land described in this study? Based on our findings, these changes and events can be expected to take place within the next century:

- Everybody will have a moustache
- The Vancouver Canucks will win zero Stanley Cups
- They'll finally finish whatever they're doing to the Trans-Canada around Kenora, ON
- Calgary will overtake Toronto in population, wealth, and Axe body spray consumption
- Rising Arctic temperatures will turn Iqaluit into a thriving hamlet

Canadians are significantly outnumbered. Our best guess is that there are probably dozens of non-Canadians for every Canadian. Despite this, our findings suggest Canadian culture is as strong as ever. Underneath the trivial coffee cup sweepstakes and hockey highlight reels exists a solid bedrock of shared history, values, and fondness for ketchup chips.

This landmark study of Canada and Canadians has shone a rare floodlight on the people, places, and pastimes that make up this sprawling tract of unwanted land. We hope that you, the reader, have enjoyed seeing yourself reflected in these articles and charts. Collecting this information has been the ultimate honour, and was worth all the long hours and mosquito bites.

Stats all, folks.

Other Books
by Stats Canada

- *Stats Canada: Where Is New Brunswick?*
- *Stats Canada: A Guide to New Brunswick*
- *Stats Canada: Pocket Guide to Salmon Arm, BC*
- *Harry Potter 3*
- *Stats Canada: The Perfect Pot of KD*
- *Stats Canada Presents: The History of Ketchup*
- *Stats Canada: For Dummies*
- *Stats America: Stats About Canada's Underpants*
- *Chicken Soup for the Canadian Soul*
- *Stats Canada: I Seriously Need More Information About New Brunswick*
- *Stats Canada: Why We Snubbed New Brunswick*
- *Stats Canada: Top-Rated Restaurants In Salmon Arm, BC*
- *Stats Canada: Learning to Yodel (Intermediate)*
- *Stats Canada: I Murdered a Drifter*
- *Stats Canada: Wait, There's a NEW Brunswick?!*
- *Stats Canada: Learn to Row*

- *Stats Canada: Row, Boy, Row*
- *Stats Canada: A Howie Mandel Autobiography*
- *Stats Canada: If I Did It*
- *Stats Canada: Cool Snowboards*
- *The Official Justin Bieber Biography*

Credits

Photo: George Brown
Source: Library and Archives Canada
Credit: Notman & Fraser/Canadian Intellectual Property Office
fonds/c011334

Print: George Etienne Cartier
Source: Library and Archives Canada/Department of External Affairs
fonds/c002728

Print: Sir A.T. Galt, K.C.M.P., Commissaire Impérial
Source: Library and Archives Canada/e010956953

Photo: Hon. James Cockburn, M.P., (Northumberland W., Ont.)
Source: Library and Archives Canada
Credit: Topley Studio fonds/a033515

Photo: John A. Macdonald
Source: Library and Archives Canada
Credit: Notman Studio/c010144

Photo: Sir Wilfrid Laurier
Source: Library and Archives Canada
Credit: William James Topley/Topley Studio fonds/a012299

Photo: Rt. Hon. W.L. Mackenzie King
Source: Library and Archives Canada/National Film Board fonds/
c013225

Photo: Rt. Hon. Pierre Elliott Trudeau – Prime Minister of Canada
(1968–1979/1979–1984) © Library and Archives Canada.
Reproduced with the permission of Library and Archives Canada.
Source: Library and Archives Canada
Credit: Duncan Cameron/Duncan Cameron fonds/e046600

Photo: Mr. Brian Mulroney and Mrs. Mila Mulroney speaking
to Prime Minister Pierre Elliott Trudeau at the gala event for the
swearing in of the Governor-General Jeanne Sauvé held at the
National Art Centre © Government of Canada. Reproduced with
the permission of the Minister of Public Works and Government
Services Canada (2013).
Source: Library and Archives Canada
Credit: Robert Cooper/a152416.

Photo: Jean Chrétien © Library and Archives Canada. Reproduced
with the permission of Library and Archives Canada.
Source: Library and Archives Canada
Credit: Duncan Cameron/Duncan Cameron fonds/e011065949.

Acknowledgments

Andrew would like to thank his loving parents, Paul and Angie, his forgiving sister, Annie, his hetero lifemate, Dave, his bearded bestie, Ren (below), his musical advisers, Joe and Brendan, his life coach, Melody, his sassy ethnic friend, Maya, and his Grade 10 Canadian history teacher, Mr. Lanspeary.

Ren would like to thank his patient girlfriend, Melody Krauze, his supportive parents, Rob and Cathy, his brother, Matt, his sister, Heather, the guys in his hockey pool, his incredible friends and creative partners in @stats_canada, and the millions of Canadians who make this country one of the two or three greatest countries in North America.

Julia would like to thank her parents, Helen Merrell and George Davidovich, her life partner, Jon Sender, and her precious sweet angel cat-son, Francis. Julia does not want to thank her brother, Richard.

Megan would like to thank her cat, Dexter, for the continued support. She would also like to thank her friends (you know who you are), her brother, Evan (who once ran her over with a GT snow racer), her grandmother Joyce, her extended family across all of Canada, and lastly her amazing parents, Debbie and George, who still don't think this book is real.

Sam would like to thank her parents for giving her character-building red hair, her TV parents, Eric and Tami Taylor, her friends who thankfully find her quirks endearing, her high school English teacher Ms. Clarke who knew she could do this, the English teacher who didn't, and Meryl Streep.

Eric would like to thank Melinda Moradipour Taylor, his unbelievably encouraging wife and mother of their beautiful daughter, Dariya Taylor. Melinda is the love of Eric's life, without whom he would have never been able to complete this book. Eric would also like to thank his mother, India Taylor, who provided him with many opportunities to laugh. Lastly, Eric would like to thank Prime Minister Stephen Harper for always being true to himself no matter what the entire country thinks of him.

The entire Stats Canada team would like to thank Carly Watters, Justin Stoller, everybody at Penguin who helped turn this book into something coherent, and the hundreds of thousands of Internet strangers who've embraced us all along.